Volume 1: Introduction & Tools

Structured Development for Real-Time Systems

YOURDON COMPUTING SERIES
Ed Yourdon, *Advisor*

Volume 1: Introduction & Tools

Structured Development for Real-Time Systems

by Paul T. Ward &
Stephen J. Mellor

YOURDON PRESS
PRENTICE HALL BUILDING
ENGLEWOOD CLIFFS, NJ 07632

Library of Congress Catalog Number 85-050815

Printed in the United States of America

10

ISBN   0-13-854787-4   025

Prentice-Hall International (UK) Limited, *London*
Prentice-Hall of Australia Pty. Limited, *Sydney*
Prentice-Hall Canada Inc., *Toronto*
Prentice-Hall Hispanoamericana, S.A., *Mexico*
Prentice-Hall of India Private Limited, *New Delhi*
Prentice-Hall of Japan, Inc., *Tokyo*
Prentice-Hall of Southeast Asia Pte. Ltd., *Singapore*
Editora Prentice-Hall do Brasil, Ltda., *Rio de Janeiro*

Dedications

To Pamela with Love

— P.T.W.

To both my families

— S.J.M.

ACKNOWLEDGMENTS

This book is the result of work that began at Yourdon, Inc. four years ago when clients from the aerospace and manufacturing industries, notably Lockheed Missile and Space, Dupont, and Foxboro, pointed to the inadequacies of a purely data-flow-oriented approach to real-time systems analysis, and a purely program-design-oriented approach to real-time systems design, At that time, the authors and Ira Morrow of the Yourdon staff began an effort to produce real-time courses. We are now teaching the third edition of a curriculum in real-time systems analysis and design.

The curriculum and this book have been immeasurably improved from these beginnings by feedback from students, other Yourdon instructors, and our consulting clients. We appreciate the questions, suggestions, and criticisms from these sources. We would especiallly like to thank Dell Campbell, Bill Robinson, Jim Clark, John Shuttleworth, Fritz Bauman, George Mazur, Steve Weiss, John Baker, Pete Coad, Dave Bulman (who suggested an alternate notation for state transition diagrams that we ultimately adopted in a modified form), Sally Shlaer (who built a control systems development environment in which modeling played a primary role), Diana Grand, Bernard Pech, Michael O'Brien, John Lynch, Dave Wilner, and the members of the ICS project team, George Shering, Pal Anderssen, and Ian Willers.

We would especially like to acknowledge the contributions of our colleague Nancy Matzke. Nan showed extraordinary patience in listening to preliminary versions of many of our ideas and provided essential refinements and clarifications.

Finally, we would like to thank Vicki Mehserle and Debbie Barnes for patiently typing the bulk of the manuscript, Kathy Jillson and Gerry Madigan for their editorial assistance, and Ed Yourdon for his continuing support and encouragement of our venture.

CONTENTS

SECTION 2: TOOLS

NOTE ON PRELIMINARY EDITION

We are publishing this preliminary edition in three volumes. The first volume serves as an introduction and describes a set of general tools for modeling the complexities of real-time systems. The second volume addresses the techniques of essential modeling (loosely, systems analysis). It shows how the tools are used to construct a model of what needs to be done. The third volume addresses the techniques of implementation modeling (loosely, system design). These techniques use the tools described in the introductory volume plus some additional tools to construct a model of the chosen solution.

We are eagerly seeking feedback from our professional colleagues on improvements in presentation and content. We intend to incorporate this feedback into a subsequent edition of this book to be published in the near future.

Authors' Preface

Real-time and embedded systems are in widespread use in the modern world. From the microprocessor controller in a camera, through "smart" traffic lights and production control systems, to large defense systems, computer technology is increasingly a part of systems that control and respond to their environments in real-time. As the technology has improved, we have come to rely on these systems more and more — we have even put our lives in their hands. Airplanes, biomedical accelerators, nuclear power plants, and the like all depend on real-time control to operate safely. A failure in a control system, such as not responding correctly to faults in the environment, could endanger many lives.

Unfortunately, we have seen a tendency for developers to focus too heavily on the intricacies of the engineering and computer technology, to the detriment of understanding the real-world problem at hand. At best, this wastes time and resources, and at worst it is dangerous in light of the life-critical nature of today's systems. We believe that this misplaced focus results at least partly from the lack of a comprehensive set of modeling tools and techniques fitted to the real-time development environment.

In this book, we provide tools and techniques for visualizing and verifying the operation of a real-time system prior to construction, and we demonstrate their usefulness. Both of us have used these tools and techniques in practice, and we are aiming squarely at other practitioners: individuals with experience in real-time system construction who are searching for a broad-based framework in which to fit their knowledge.

Our practical orientation has influenced our approach to references. We have attempted to be scrupulous in citing our indebtedness to the work of others, and have referenced parallel developments where we felt comparisons would be helpful to the developer. However, this book is is in no sense a survey of the field, and the academic reader will need to look elsewhere for comprehensive set of references.

SECTION 1
INTRODUCTION

The five chapters of the first section serve to introduce the major issues in modeling real-time systems.

Chapter 1 examines the historical phases of systems development, and shows that developing real-time systems is becoming a discipline dominated by the problem to be solved rather that by the technology used in the solution.

Chapter 2 gives the characteristics of real-time systems, thus describing the systems within the scope of this book. On-line interactive systems are not discussed, although the tools and techniques described herein can be applied to such systems.

Chapter 3 describes the requirements for a system modeling language for real-time systems.

Chapter 4 introduces the idea of modeling heuristics — rules of thumb used in modeling a system — and introduces two fundamental heuristics.

Finally, Chapter 5 describes an overall scheme for systems development: a systems development life cycle. Although the life cycle must be tailored for each project, this book follows the basic sequence of activities laid out in this chapter.

1
Historical Perspective

1.1 Historical phases in engineering disciplines

The old adage — "everybody talks about the weather, but nobody does anything about it" [1] — has recently been proven false. People are indeed doing something about the weather; they are anticipating its short-term variations fairly effectively. Such anticipation (for example, the prediction that a hurricane will strike a land area) has undoubtedly saved thousands of lives and millions of dollars in property. A less dramatic consequence is that millions of us routinely use the nightly newspaper, radio, or television weather forecast to plan our activities for the following day.

Although weather forecasting owes much to discoveries in the pure and applied sciences, we want to explore its engineering aspects; in other words, the fashioning of effective systems for weather prediction. Let's differentiate between the essential formulation of the problem, the qualitative aspects of the implementation technology, and the quantitative aspects of the implementation technology.

The formulation of the problem is as follows: given a set of actual meteorological variable values $M_a(R,T)$ sampled within a region R and a time interval T, calculate the expected values $M_e(R,T+\delta T)$ of a subset of these variables in a subset of the same region within a time interval greater by δT (say by one day). The acceptance criterion for the expected values is that for a specified percentage of these calculations: $|M_{ai}(R,T+\delta T) - M_{ei}(R,T+\delta T)| <$ some measure of error e_i for each variable M_i in the set. For example, it might be required that the average temperature over the time interval be predicted to within 5 degrees Centigrade 85 percent of the time.

Given this formulation of the problem, the implementation technology required for its solution must have certain qualitative characteristics. Sensors capable of measuring the meteorological variables must be available, an algorithm for calculating the M_e as a function of the M_a must be devised, a processor capable of carrying out the algorithm must exist, and a communications network to carry the M_a to the processor must be available.

Finally, the implementation technology must obey a specific quantitative constraint: the time to convey the M_a to the processor plus the time to perform the calculation must be less than δT. In other words, a system that takes 48 hours to produce a 24-hour forecast wouldn't be of much use.

There are several interesting relationships between the technology and the problem formulation. For example, the non-existence of sensors (human or mechanical) to measure the M_a would make the system impossible to implement. On the other hand, an algorithm that was less than perfect would allow an implementation *if some distortion in the problem formulation was allowed*. For instance, it might make sense to accept larger deviations between expected and actual variables or a lower percentage of successes. Such distortion, of course, has intrinsic limitations. Beyond a certain point the calculations of expected values would not be significantly better than guesses.

Let's now focus on a very specific relation between the technology and the problem formulation for weather prediction. Prior to the nineteen forties, all the qualitative aspects of the technology were in existence. Sensors to sample the weather data were available, and the mathematics of weather prediction had been worked out [2]. Furthermore, since most mathematical calculations can be approximated by simple arithmetic operations, people with mechanical calculators (or even with paper and pencil) could perform calculations of the type required. Despite all of this, quantitative constraints made the problem insoluble in a practical sense. There was no feasible way of organizing an army of clerks with calculators to perform a weather prediction calculation within a reasonable time.

The advent of electronic digital computers changed the situation radically. At the Institute for Advanced Study, the time required for a 24-hour forecast was reduced from 24 hours in 1949 to 6 minutes in 1953 [3]. As the technological threshold was being approached and crossed, the situation was similar to that described earlier concerning the less-than-perfect algorithm. Successful implementations were in reach *if the problem formulation could be compromised to reflect technological limitations.* It is reasonable to characterize such a development process as being *implementation dominated.*

Now that we've examined an engineering process as it crossed a technological threshold, let's use another illustration to explore the situation where the capabilities of a technology far exceed the requirements of the average problem. Imagine that a reasonably affluent person wants a custom-built house. The problem formulation will be worked out by consultation with an architect and will no doubt specify esthetic and social criteria for an acceptable product, with the more fundamental criterion of adequate shelter simply taken for granted. In working out the plans for the builder, the architect typically has an embarassment of riches — a variety of available building technologies able to satisfy the problem formulation.

The process of specifying, designing, and building a modern house is clearly *problem dominated.* One can, of course, visualize an implementation-dominated era in the history of human shelter provision. Picture a prehistoric tribe living in a treeless area where caves are to be found. The clearing of accumulated debris from a cave is the only technology for providing shelter, and any disadvantages of cave-dwelling are accepted as inevitable.

There are many other examples like those just discussed; it seems that a historical cycle can be traced for many engineering disciplines. In the earliest phase of the cycle, adequate technology to solve a particular type of problem simply doesn't exist.* Problem formulations either aren't attempted or are considered of only theoretical interest. The next phase is one in which a technology becomes just barely capable of solving a type of problem. The engineering of solutions in this phase is inevitably implementation dominated, and the engineering point of view can be characterized as, How can the

---

* There are obviously cases in which the technology exists but where its cost is so high (or its reliability so low) as to exceed any possible benefit to the end user. We consider this equivalent to the non-existence of a technology.

problem be changed to fit the available solution. A third phase of the cycle occurs as the implementation technology becomes more powerful, or as alternative technologies are invented. During this phase, the class of soluble problems increases, and the technology becomes more than adequate to solve the average problem. The engineering approach shifts in a corresponding fashion from implementation dominated to problem dominated. The final phase may be thought of as the maturity of the engineering discipline. The engineering approach is completely problem dominated. The fitting of existing technologies to new problems and the development of new technologies focus on such secondary characteristics as cost and flexibility rather than on the solubility of problems.

Although this idea of historical phases provides a useful perspective, it ignores a critical factor that we'll explore in the next section.

1.2 Mismatches between approach and historical phase

An unspoken assumption throughout the last section was that the engineering approach was well matched to the historical phase of the discipline. In other words, we assumed that the engineer could recognize the state of the available technology versus the problem at hand and adopt an implementation-dominated or problem-dominated approach accordingly. Clearly this is not always the case. Let's explore the two obvious extremes — taking a problem-dominated approach when the technology is inadequate, and taking an implementation-dominated approach when the technology is mature. We'll examine the history of on-line business systems for illustrations of both types of problem.

When reliable video display terminals became commercially available in the early nineteen seventies, many businesses saw the potential of these terminals for making information more accessible to their employees. The typical large business at that time stored large amounts of data on disk files and produced voluminous weekly reports on paper concerning inventories, customer orders, and so on. Since the data changed daily, these reports lost their usefulness as the week progressed, and there was a need for more up-to-date data. The idea of a clerk being able to key in an inventory item number and to see a current available balance displayed, for example, was extremely attractive.

Despite the promise of the technology, many early attempts at on-line systems were dismal failures because of excessive response times. The system developers, through misinformation or inexperience, failed to anticipate that although the available technology was *qualitatively adequate* (it could display stored data on demand), it was *quantitatively inadequate* (it could not provide adequate response times in a multi-user environment). In terms of our previous classification, a problem-dominated approach (providing access to all up-to-date inventory data for all employees) was taken when a technology-dominated approach (which pieces of inventory data can be made available to which employees without overloading the system) was required.

For most routine applications, rapidly evolving on-line technology made more comprehensive systems feasible within a few years. Businesses began using video display terminals for entry of customer order and inventory transactions as well as for inquiries on data values. Some of these on-line data entry systems, however, had a characteristic that was puzzling and often annoying to the users. The data for a transaction had to be entered in segments, each of which consisted of eighty or fewer letters or numbers. The reason for this feature? The internal handling of these transactions was derived from earlier systems in which data entered and left on eighty-column punch cards! In this case, an implementation-dominated approach (transactions must be divided into eighty-column chunks) was used instead of a problem-dominated approach, which would have identified a natural organization of parts for each transaction.

The critical factor, then, is a mismatch between development approach and historical phase. Now that we've examined some instances of this problem in business-oriented software engineering, let's take a broader perspective.

1.3 Historical phases of business systems engineering

Businesses have been using complex machines for data processing since the latter part of the nineteenth century. However, the earlier technologies (typewriters, mechanical calculators, punched-card-handling machines) could solve only business problems of quite limited scope. The linking of these mechanized implementations into business-wide systems required interfaces for data storage and data preparation that are human-labor-intensive.

The advent of digital computers in the nineteen forties made available technologies that were many orders of magnitude more powerful than those used in earlier business machines. An examination of any of a number of common business areas (payroll or inventory control, for example) shows the now-familiar trend of technology maturing and becoming able to solve most routine problems. However, the possibility of a misfit between the development approach and the maturity of the technology, which we discussed earlier, makes the trend much less clear in the actual practice of the average systems developer.

There are certainly some generalizations that can be made about the evolution of systems-development methods. As an illustration, the rise of "user friendliness" as a criterion for a successful implementation shows a clear shift toward a problem-dominated approach to the engineering of business systems. Not only have user-friendly application systems been created, but also there have been attempts at user-friendly system software, such as UNIX[R] [4].

The trend from early, technologically primitive interfaces to later, user-friendly interfaces has also repeated itself on various types of hardware. The evolutionary process is clearly visible in the case of microprocessor-based personal computers. In fact, the problem-dominated and technology-dominated approaches are currently in open conflict. Lee Felsenstein, the designer of the Osborne 1, recently objected to the implementation of UNIX[R] on personal computers because "UNIX[R] is a bloated operating system designed to run bloated programs on bloated computers" [5]; in other words, because it uses the technology inefficiently.

One method for studying evolving engineering practices in systems development is to examine the technical literature. Such an examination divulges the following two clear trends:

● As automated technology has matured, ad-hoc development practices have been superceded by more formal approaches.

- As automated technology has matured, the scope of the formal practices has widened from focusing on implementation methods to encompassing problem formulation.

Neither of these trends is surprising, given the relationships between problems and implementation technologies discussed earlier in this chapter.

As a specific example, let's examine the evolution of formal methods for software development. The earliest papers of interest were concerned with a discipline for programming. The acknowledged pioneers in this area were Bohm and Jacopini [6] and Dijkstra [7]. The developed methods ultimately came to be called *structured programming,* and consisted of a set of guidelines for coding designed to maximize the clarity and maintainability of groups of computer instructions. Implicit in structured programming is the assumption that various organizations of instructions can be used to implement a single calculation, and that the criterion for choosing among organizations is *not* optimum performance — a sure sign of the evolution of the technology away from the implementation-dominated phase.

Another major step in software development was announced in pivotal papers by Stevens, Myers, and Constantine [8], and Parnas [9]; *structured design* and *information hiding* provide a set of quality-assurance criteria for the relationships among independently addressable groups of instructions (modules). This approach permits organizing much larger groups of instructions than was practical with only the guidelines of structured programming. Since the methods of structured design prescribe a subroutine call protocol among the modules — a practice not conducive to optimum performance — they represent a step further away from an implementation-dominated approach.

Both structured programming and structured design are implementation disciplines, which assume that computer instructions are being organized to satisfy a well-defined requirement. Another step forward was the development of *structured analysis* by Ross [10] and others. Structured analysis provides a method for building a somewhat formal and rigorous requirements-definition model. DeMarco [11], in fact, specifically designates the model as an input to the structured-design process — a clear indication that the problem formulation is intended to drive the implementation and not vice versa.

Note that we have included the formal techniques for programming, design, and analysis within the section on business systems. None of these disciplines has specifically restricted itself to use in business systems. However, the vast majority of the uses of these techniques have been in typical business applications. In the next section, we will examine the history of real-time systems development.

1.4 Historical phases of real-time systems engineering

We have not yet attempted to characterize real-time systems; the common-sense definition of the domain includes applications such as avionics (automatic pilots, flight management) and industrial process control.

As with business applications, the use of technology for these real-time applications antedates the availability of electronic digital computers. Many closed-loop control systems were (and still are) implemented with electrical or pneumatic analog devices. However, the development of modern computer technology enabled the solving of larger and more complex problems. As the technology matured, both techniques from the business-systems sphere and techniques developed for analog process-control engineering were adapted in an ad-hoc fashion to the engineering of digital electronic real-time systems. However, formal development techniques fitted to the real-time environment evolved slowly. Only recently, as with business systems, have formal problem-formulation techniques [12, 13, 14, 15, 16] been proposed.

The acceptance of formal methods for real-time systems development has been slower than in the case of business systems. We believe that this reluctance has been caused by two factors. The first factor is that the quantitative demands on the technology (for example, processor speed requirements) have been much more stringent for typical real-time applications than for typical business applications. Not until the explosive growth of microprocessor capabilities in the late nineteen seventies was it possible to shift from an implementation-dominated to a problem-dominated approach to development. The second factor is that the intrinsic complexity of typical real-time problems exceeds that of typical business problems, making a comprehensive development approach more difficult to create.

We believe the time is now ripe for problem-dominated approaches to the engineering of real-time systems. Current computer technology has ample capability to solve a large set of typical real-time problems. Furthermore, the formal development techniques that have evolved in the business-systems environment provide a useful base from which real-time methods can evolve. The remainder of the book will be devoted to explaining and illustrating the use of a problem-dominated approach to real-time systems development.

1.5 Summary

An effective approach to systems development requires evaluating the capabilities of the technology and the nature of the problem and choosing an approach dominated either by the problem or by the technology. The capabilities of existing technology suggest that a problem-dominated approach is appropriate for many real-time systems development tasks.

The next chapter will explain the scope of our use of the term "real-time" to characterize a system.

Chapter 1: References

1. C.D. Warner. Editorial. *Hartford Courant (Conn.), August 24, 1897.*

2. L.F. Richardson. *Weather Prediction by Numerical Process,* Dover Edition, 1966.

3. H.H. Goldstine. *The Computer: from Pascal to von Neumann.* Princeton University Press, 1972, pp.303-304.

4. *The UNIX Programmer's Manual* Murray Hill, N.J.: Bell Telephone Laboratories, 1973.

5. J. Markoff. "Can Unix Ever Fit Personal Computers?" *Info World,* 5/5 - 6/1 (December 1983 - January 1985), pp.40-42.

6. C. Bohm and G. Jacopini. "Flow Diagrams, Turing Machines and Languages with Only Two Formation Rules." *Communications of the ACM,* Vol. 9, No. 5 (May 1966), pp.366-71.

7. E. Dijkstra, "Go To Statement Considered Harmful." *Communications of the ACM,* Vol. 11, No. 3 (May 1966), pp.147-48.

8. W. Stevens, G. Myers, and L. Constantine. "Structured Design," *IBM Systems Journal,* Vol. 13, No. 2 (May 1974), pp.115-39.

9. D.L. Parnas, "On the Criteria to Be Used in Decomposing Systems into Modules." *Communications of the ACM,* Vol. 5.,No. 12 (December 1972), pp.1053-58.

10. D.T. Ross and K.E. Schoman, Jr. "Structured Analysis for Requirements Definition." *IEEE Transactions on Software Engineering* (January 1977) Vol.SE-3, No.5, pp. 6-15.

11. T. DeMarco *Structured Analysis and System Specification.* Yourdon Press, 1978, pp.314-15.

12. D.L. Parnas, "The Use of Precise Specifications in the Development of Software." *Information Processing 77.* Proceedings of the International Federation of Information Processing Congresses, New York, 1977.

13. K.L. Heninger. "Specifying Software Requirements for Complex Systems: New Techniques and their Application." *IEEE Transactions on Software Engineering,* Vol. SE-6 (January 1980), pp.2-13.

14. M.W. Alford. "A Requirements Engineering Methodology for Real-Time Processing Requirements." *IEEE Transactions on Software Engineering.* Vol. SE-3, No. 5 (January 1977).

15. P. Zave, "The Operational Approach to Software Development." Paper Presented at the Rocky Mountain Institute of Software Engineering, Aspen, July 1984.

16 P. Ward and D. Campbell, "Structured Analysis for Process Control Systems." Presented at ISA, Houston, October 1983.

2
Characterization of Real-Time Systems

2.1 Scope, environment, and vocabulary

It should be clear from the preceding chapter that this book will emphasize the distinction between the formulation of a systems development problem and the choice of technology to implement a solution. Although this approach is firmly embedded in the folklore of human problem solving (the differentiation of ends from means, for example), it is not simple to formulate a clear set of guidelines for distinguishing elements of a problem from elements of a solution.

Part of the difficulty stems from the arbitrary nature of the definition of a system. The primary definition of the term *system* as given by the College Edition of the Random House Dictionary of the English Language is "an assemblage or combination of things or parts forming a complex or unitary whole." The universe is full of "things and parts," so any method of pointing to a subset of the universe and distinguishing it from the whole defines a system. Systems definition, then, establishes an imaginary boundary and places the system inside the boundary and the remainder of the universe outside as the environment. It is impossible to distinguish between the essentials of a problem and the formulation of a solution unless this boundary is carefully defined.

As an example, consider a bank clerk entering transactions and obtaining the results of those transactions through a video display terminal connected to a mainframe computer containing transaction-processing tasks and a database. If a boundary is drawn so that the video display terminal and the mainframe constitute the system, the bank clerk is excluded and becomes the system's environment. From the clerk's point of view, then, one can formulate a problem of "devising a system for recording and displaying the results of banking transactions." This formulation clearly puts the terminal and the mainframe into the category of implementation technology; a manual ledger system would also be a solution to this problem. Now imagine that the imaginary boundary is changed so that it lies between the mainframe and the terminal, with the terminal considered to be the system's environment. (Since the clerk does not interact directly with the mainframe, he or she is invisible to the system as defined here.) The problem may now be formulated as "accepting banking transactions from and returning results to a video display terminal." This drastically changes the range of possible implementations; although a minicomputer might be substituted for the mainframe, a non-automated solution is no longer possible with this choice of boundary.

Changes in system boundaries are intimately bound up with changes in the vocabulary used in problem formulation. In the example just given, the version of the system with the bank clerk as the environment has a natural vocabulary and problem description drawn from banking terminology. A more detailed problem formulation, from the clerk's point of view, would certainly use terms such as *deposit, balance,* and *account number.* Introducing terms such as *transmission rate* or *parity checking* clearly would be venturing into the realm of the implementation. On the other hand, putting the display terminal in the environment makes it impossible to formulate the problem without introducing vocabulary drawn from display-terminal technology. In fact, the vocabulary used might be a hybrid of banking terms and display-terminal terms. It will be shown later in the chapter that such a hybrid vocabulary can be a sign of a poorly chosen system definition.

Keeping the relationships between system boundaries, system environments, and problem-definition vocabularies in mind, we will now attempt to characterize the type of system we think of as "real-time."

2.2 An inventory of real-time characteristics

The problem-formulation vocabulary for real-time systems is drawn from science and engineering disciplines. The natural environment of a real-time system is the scientist, engineer, or technician and his or her technology. We expect to see real-time problems formulated in language drawn from biophysics, industrial chemistry, mechanical engineering, or geology rather than in terms of banking, insurance, or inventory control. Notice that, although computers are ubiquitous in scientific and engineering applications, the intrinsic vocabulary of a discipline such as chemistry is clearly distinguishable from the vocabulary of automated hardware and software. This vocabulary distinction is significant since, as shown in the previous section, it is correlated with the separation of the problem formulation and the details of implementation in systems development problems.

One area of potential difficulty in this regard concerns systems that perform technical support functions in an automated environment. A logic analyzer, for example, which monitors the performance of the microprocessor to which it is attached, is typically implemented with microprocessor components. In such a case, the problem-formulation and problem-implementation vocabularies are quite similar, and care must be exercised to keep them separate.

The environment of a real-time system often contains devices that act as the senses of the system. In a broad sense any system that accepts input may be said to be sensing what is occurring in its environment. However, non-real-time systems are restricted to inputs that occur at discrete points in time and are highly structured (for example, keyboard or data line inputs). A real-time system, on the other hand, is typically attached to sensors such as thermocouples, optical scanners, and contact probes, and can thus collect a continuous stream of relatively unstructured data. This is analogous to the functioning of the senses in a living creature – one might say that real-time systems can have skin, eyes, taste buds, and so on.

The environment of a real-time system also often contains devices that can effect physical changes as sensory inputs occur. Any system that produces outputs, of course, makes changes in its environment. However, the outputs of a real-time system often are continuous in character and overlap the continuous inputs from the sensors – thus the operation of a real-time system often mimics human patterns such as eye-hand coordination. Such a system also changes the physical world in a quite literal way – by changing temperatures, valve positions, and so on – rather than in the more abstract way of merely producing information to be acted on.

Real-time systems often require concurrent processing of multiple inputs. Nearly all non-trivial systems require inputs from multiple sources, and these inputs may be overlapped in on-line interactive implementations. Nevertheless, true requirements for concurrency usually involve correlated processing of two or more inputs over the same time interval and are quite different in character from the overlapping of transactions in a multi-user interactive business system. An industrial process control system, for example, might be required to correlate values of the temperature, pressure, and concentration of a chemical reaction and to perform simultaneous adjustments of heaters and valves to maintain a reaction in a desired state. On the other hand, a system handling on-line inquiries from two users that are entered at about the same time need not be truly concurrent – although it may be implemented in that way -- but must merely respond to both transactions within a short time interval.

Please note that it is often possible to satisfy a concurrent processing requirement with a non-concurrent implementation. A single task on a single processor can simulate monitoring of concurrent inputs by repetition of a sampling sequence. Choosing such a single-task, single-processor strategy has specific advantages and also has characteristic disadvantages, such as the need for trial-and-error code optimization to meet timing constraints. It is important not to mistake the characteristics of a specific implementation strategy with characteristics of the problem itself. Monitoring of concurrently present inputs can be accomplished by allocating a microprocessor chip to each input or by running one task per input on a set of one or more processors controlled by an operating system, as well as by one task on one processor. Each of these approaches has costs and benefits; before any implementation approach is chosen, the problem should be well-understood.

The time scales of many real-time systems are fast by human standards. In terms of exchange of information between human beings or between human beings and automated systems, one second is not a long delay. The devices that real-time systems monitor and control, on the other hand, often operate on time scales in which one second is an extremely long time. As an example, consider an automobile cruise-control system. In order to maintain a smooth ride with only small variations from the desired speed, the actual speed must be monitored many times per second. Although this is rapid by human standards, it is on the low end of the spectrum in terms of real-time requirements.

With respect to system-environment interactions, the time scales of real-time systems are much closer to the operating speeds of available implementation technology than are the time scales of other automated systems. Thus typical real-time systems for many years pushed the limits of the available automated hardware and software, and, as mentioned in the last chapter, this phenomenon slowed the evolution from implementation-oriented to problem-oriented development approaches.

The precision of response required of real-time systems is greater than that required of other systems. Consider a system that must begin receiving and recording a radio transmission 2 seconds after receiving a control signal. The required speed of response is quite similar to that of demanding on-line inquiry applications. However, variations of 1.5 seconds from the norm (responses as short as 0.5 second or as long as 3.5 seconds) would not be a problem in most on-line inquiry systems. Variations of the order of the response time would clearly be unacceptable in the radio transmission case.

Please understand that the list of characteristics just given does not constitute a definition; a system need not have all of these characteristics to be considered a real-time system. A given system may be clearly in the real-time category and be lacking requirements for concurrency, as in the example of a single-loop process control system. Similarly, a system that does not produce physical changes in its environment, such as one that displays instantaneous values of process variables to an operator, can be distinctly real-time in character.

The significance of the list above is that a systems-development formalism that is usable in a real-time development environment must be powerful enough to describe a system with all of these characteristics.

There is a class of important systems that is commonly called "real-time" but possesses few if any of the characteristics listed above. This is the subject of the next section.

2.3 Real-time systems versus on-line interactive systems

It is common to refer to systems that operate in an on-line, interactive environment and that require fast response times as "real-time systems." While we have no desire to institute a wholesale reform in nomenclature, it is important to point out how these systems differ from the kinds of systems that we will address in this book.

Consider the banking problem, introduced in section 1 of this chapter, from the point of view of the clerk: recording and reporting on banking transactions. Such a problem formulation would often be accompanied by a quantitative constraint, such as "report the result of a transaction within two seconds." The problem formulation certainly does not qualify as "real-time," and the quantitative constraint qualifies only in terms of response time, if at all.

The "real-time" designation in a system of this type arises because of the typical *implementation* strategy. It is common for a number of bank clerks to work at video display terminals connected to a single mainframe processor, and to enter transactions during the same time period. From the point of view of the mainframe, the situation has a number of real-time characteristics, as follows:

- The problem of communicating between a mainframe and a display terminal must be formulated at least partly in communications-engineering terms (baud rate, parity checking).

- The mainframe may be sending and receiving banking transactions from a number of terminals concurrently.

- The response time can be quite fast in terms of total number of banking transactions per second.

- The precision of response required will be considerable in terms of synchronizing banking data sent and received on terminal transmission lines.

Notice that the problem as just described results from a shift of system boundary to put the terminal in the environment. It was mentioned in section 1 that there is a potential problem with this choice of boundary. One way to approach this problem is to observe that first, the banking problem isn't real-time from the point of view of an individual clerk and second, it isn't real-time from the point of view of a designer or implementer *provided that an adequate software architecture is available.* For example, in a CICS environment a programmer need only write a piece of COBOL code with the appropriate CICS input/output statements, and the system software will deal with the real-time aspects of the problem.

The point is that choosing the system boundary between the terminal and the mainframe for a banking system invites the mixing of two problems that can be better handled separately. There is a banking problem (specifying transaction-processing details) that is best described in banking terms from the point of view of a clerk and that has nothing to do with real-time issues, and there is a system software problem (working out a mechanism for mainframe-to-terminal communication) that has nothing to do with banking but that may well be real-time in character. (Notice that the term "banking" is superfluous in the bulleted list of points earlier in this section.)

The discussion above does not imply the absence of real-time problems in the banking environment. The inadequacy of existing system software or the necessity of creating a customized implementation environment may well require employees of a bank's data processing department to deal with real-time systems problems. Such problems are best addressed, however, by separating the systems completely from the applications they will serve when completed.

Finally, please note that while we shall not address on-line systems (such as the banking system) in this book, the system development formalism we propose is sufficiently general to address problems of this type.

3
Real-Time Modeling Issues

3.1 The nature of models

One of the essentials of the highly evolved social organization of the human species is our ability to communicate using symbols. Our spoken and written languages constitute an elaborate model of the realities surrounding us, a model that allows us to exchange complex information about people, places, and things without actually needing to see or touch them. The converse is also true: any model is a language whose symbols allow us to exchange information without actual contact with the things modeled. Although natural language is incomparably rich as a model, people throughout the ages have felt the need to create narrower, more specialized models or languages for certain purposes. For example, algebraic notation has evolved because the written word is not a particularly effective way for one person to tell another about complex quantitative relationships.

Modeling inevitably involves a process of abstraction; a symbol cannot represent *all* the aspects of the thing for which it stands. To use again the analogy of algebra, let's compare a particular relationship between numeric values, say 3 and 5, with the general algebraic expression $X < Y$. The specific details of the relationship between 3 and 5, such as the value of the difference, are lost because of the general nature of the algebraic notation. This quality of abstraction is not a defect of the modeling process; on the contrary, suppressing details removes distractions and allows concentration on the essentials.

To say that the abstraction process can be beneficial is not to say that it is always beneficial. Presumably, the well-established uses of symbols (spoken and written language, algebraic notation) have developed by trial-and-error, so that they are well fitted to their environments. It is said, for example, that the languages of arctic-dwellers have a much more elaborate vocabulary for describing snow than do the languages used in more temperate climates. If a new ice age were to descend on North America, we English, French, and Spanish speakers might be at a disadvantage, since distinguishing precisely among varieties of snow could be important to survival. By using a term that is too general, we lose potentially valuable information.

The comparison of vocabularies for describing snow brings up another important point. Imagine displaying to an average North American three varieties of snow and asking, What do you see here? The answer would very likely be that the person sees three identical things. Our models -- the symbol systems that we use -- not only limit our possibilities for communication but also affect our very perceptions. There is no doubt that our average North American has the sensory equipment to detect differences between the three kinds of snow, but simply ignores those differences when making observations. People tend to perceive the world in terms of the symbol systems they have inherited. The symbol system thus exerts a powerful but largely invisible influence on our thinking processes — an idea expressed by Marshall McLuhan as "The medium is the message."[1]

The snow example illustrates that a change in external conditions (an ice age) can make a symbol system less suited to its environment. The symbol system has been developed for a different environment, and it hasn't had the opportunity to undergo the slow, trial-and-error selection process required for a good fit. We contend that the infrequency of use of formal methods in real-time systems development is caused by the fact that many of these methods don't fit the real-time environment well enough. In other words, people have been perceiving real-time systems and communicating about them under the largely unrecognized influences of an inadequate symbol system.

A model that doesn't fit its environment well can evolve to a better fit. Let's now examine in more detail the way in which this happens.

3.2 Evolution of models

Robert Block has observed, "Organizations want systems, not projects." [2] In other words, the less systems development, the better. This idea, of course, can easily be abused — a premature rush to implementation without adequate planning typically produces unsatisfactory systems — but the basic premise is sound. A prime criterion for a satisfactory systems-modeling language (language is used here in the sense of any medium for expressing and communicating ideas) is that it minimizes the time and effort required to develop a satisfactory system.

In the broadest sense, systems development entails the translation of a need in the minds of one or more people into a working system which meets that need. The ideal systems development approach would permit an instantaneous leap from perceived need (problem) to working system (implementation). More realistically, any modeling language that shortens the distance beween conception and implementation must be of value. To illustrate this idea, let's look at the class of systems that perform calculations on scalars, vectors, and matrices subject to constraints on the values that these may assume. Let's assume the initial conception of such a system is in algebraic terms and that the implementation will take the form of machine-language instructions in the memory of a digital processor. Clearly, the translation of a complex mathematical formula into binary digits (which was the only available option on the first digital processors) is tedious and error-prone. The use of an assembler language simplifies the task by the reducing the number of instructions that must be written, but the form of the implementation is still quite remote from the conception of the problem. The use of FORTRAN or an equivalent language produces a dramatic simplification of the work; the instructions to the digital processor can be formulated directly in algebraic terms. Finally, the use of Ada (registered trademark of the U.S. Department of Defense) with its strong typing facilities simplifies the task further by allowing range constraints to be incorporated into data definitions rather than coded as procedures. The progression from machine language to assembler language to FORTRAN to Ada represents a steady increase in the power of the modeling language and a corresponding decrease in development time and effort for the mathematically minded end-user. This same trend may be seen in many other types of models.

Let's now move from looking at a specific modeling language to considering modeling languages in general. The next four sections of this chapter will deal with desirable characteristics of such a language; the final sections will deal with what needs to be modeled in a real-time system.

3.3   Representation of systems in graphic terms

The set of desired systems, of course, is much broader than the set of desired algebraic computations, and ease of expressing mathematical manipulations is only one of the criteria for a satisfactory modeling language. The designers of Ada, in fact, made a conscious attempt to narrow the gap between conception and implementation for a broad range of systems features in addition to the mathematical ones just mentioned. Despite some clear improvements over previous languages, however, Ada suffers from a disadvantage as a general-purpose language for systems development. It is cast in the mold of traditional programming languages in that its symbol set is limited to characters and in that its syntax permits only concatenation of these characters into linear sequences. In other words, Ada does not allow the description of systems in graphic form. It thus fails to take advantage of the inherent capabilities of pictures to convey effectively complex information.

The issue here does not concern the basic representational capabilities of Ada — graphic notations are convertible into equivalent string-orientated linear notations and vice versa — but its user acceptability: its ability to facilitate the transfer of concepts into implementations. Two engineers discussing a complex problem will very often resort to drawing each other pictures in order to clarify the concepts involved. If a graphic modeling language is capable of formalization, it provides all the advantages of a text-orientated language plus some additional advantages. (A graphics-oriented language must obviously have a textual subset.) The paradigm for the modeling process should not be the entry of programming language instructions into a text-oriented work station, but should rather be the entry of graphic descriptions into the graphics-oriented CAD/CAM work station designed for circuit board and mechanical component developers.

3.4   Simplicity versus adequacy

A prime characteristic of any symbol system must be that it is *rich* enough for you to say what you need to say. Imagine, for example, that the English language contained nouns but no adjectives or prepositional phrases, and that you had to tell someone which box to select from a roomful of boxes. Without the ability to specify "the large green box" or "the box in the far corner," you would be reduced to pointing in order to communicate your meaning.

Many of the symbol systems traditionally used in systems development have inadequacies of this sort. The flowchart, for example, can describe time relationships between processes only in terms of *sequence*. Given two things A and B that must happen, it is possible to "say" using a flowchart only that A must precede B or that A must follow B; without modifying the standard notations one cannot "say" that A and B must happen *concurrently*. Thus from our point of view the flowchart hasn't a rich enough symbol system for describing real-time systems, where concurrency is often a factor. This is not to say that there's anything intrinsically wrong with a flowchart; in the restricted environment for which it was devised it's quite useful. However, systems developers who have tried to make the standard flowchart a tool for modeling real-time systems have ventured into the arctic regions with only a single word for snow.

Having made a case for richness in a symbol system, we must now take the opposite tack and admit that a rich symbol system has substantial problems associated with it. Anyone who has attempted to become fluent in a second language as an adult has encountered these problems. It is very frustrating to know exactly what you want to say, but not to know the words or the grammatical construction required to say it. A rich symbol system requires a substantial investment of time and energy to learn. Since the modeling notations used to describe systems are of only limited usefulness in everyday life, it is impractical to make them rich in symbols and therefore more difficult to learn. An ideal modeling notation from this point of view would be one that allowed a person to look *through* the notation and focus on the thing represented with minimal learning time.

The flowchart that we criticized a few paragraphs back scores very well in terms of simplicity. To appreciate this, note that one of the simplest possible models is a *graph* as the mathematicians use the term, consisting of points (nodes) to represent things and line segments (arcs) to represent connections. The flowchart is very close to this node-and-arc level of simplicity, since it fundamentally uses only two kinds of nodes (rectangles to represent processes and diamonds to represent decisions) in addition to its connecting line segments.

We seem to have encountered a dilemma. Both *notational adequacy* (a symbol system rich enough to say what must be said) and *notational simplicity* are desirable characteristics of a modeling notation, but they conflict. Fortunately, there are ways to resolve the dilemma. To illustrate the nature of one solution, we'll use the example of modeling the electrical and water connections among appliances in a house. Since some appliances use both electricity and water, the electrical and water systems aren't completely separable. However, drawing both systems on a single diagram would require either using two different symbols for the two kinds of connections (electrical and water) or labeling the connections to show which kind they were, and the resulting diagram would be quite hard to read for a complex set of connections. Our model of this situation is shown in Figures 3.1 and 3.2. By showing the two types of connections on two separate models, we have reduced the overall visual complexity that would have resulted from a single model and have also allowed the use of the same symbol to represent both electrical and water connections. (You can tell from the context of the diagram what the symbol represents.) We have also used the same symbol to represent all the appliances, distinguishing them by labels. Finally, we have maintained the integration of the two models by representing the appliances that use electricity and water on both models. This *controlled redundancy* makes it easy to see how the two models fit together to represent the entire system.

We will use all of the strategies illustrated above -- separation of models, combination of text and graphics, contextual interpretation of the meaning of symbols, and controlled redundancy -- in our approach to real-time systems development.

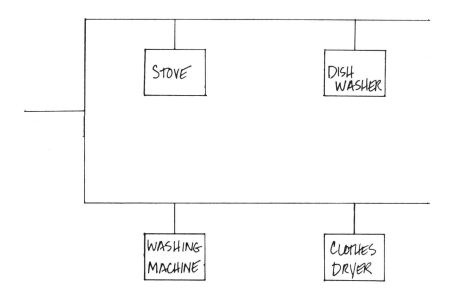

Figure 3.1. Electrical connections.

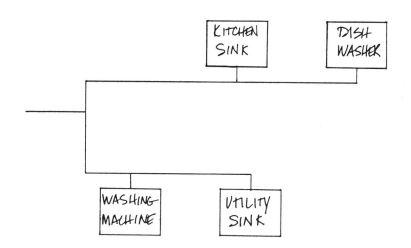

Figure 3.2. Water connections.

3.5 Management of complexity

A criterion for any systems-modeling language is that it permit representation of a system of arbitrarily great complexity. A somewhat more subtle but equally significant criterion is that the resulting representation be manageable in human terms. As with the need for graphic capabilities described in section 3.3, this latter point is not a matter of notational adequacy but of user acceptability.

Since human limitations prevent us from keeping all the details of a complex system in our heads at one time, the modeling language must allow partitioning of a system into a large number of chunks. However, it is also necessary for humans to be able to perceive in some sense a system as a whole. Thus the system must be capable of representations at various levels of detail, with the upper-level ones hiding some of the details of the lower-level ones; and it must permit a bookkeeping scheme to show the relationship of the lower-level to the higher-level representations.

We feel that management of complexity requires two distinct subsets of a modeling language. The first subset, which we call *schematic,* is capable of representing the overall plan or layout of a system or one of its parts. The other subset, which we call *specific,* can describe the detailed structure of the elemental pieces of which the system is composed. The schematic and specific portions of the notation must be integrated so that the schematic portion serves as a "graphic table of contents" for the lower-level details described by the specific portion.

In addition to a notation that permits representation at various levels of detail, a modeling language must have rules that permit the determination of whether two representations at different levels of detail are consistent.

3.6 Rigor of representation

There is a substantial difference between a model built by a systems developer to guide the construction of a man-made system and a model built by a scientist to understand the behavior of a natural system. However, there are some important similarities, which relate to the judgments made by scientists as to the usefulness of a model.

As an example, let's take the law of universal gravitation, which states that the gravitational force between two bodies is directly proportional to the product of their masses and inversely proportional to the square of the distance between them. The formula is a model of an actual system consisting of two masses.

One criterion of a useful scientific model is that, in fact, it predicts the behavior of real systems — it is capable of simulating the operation of a system. Since all models are abstractions, the degree of capability for predicting must be qualified; for example, the model might predict the behavior under certain conditions within certain tolerances, for a certain range of variables. With these qualifications a test of the gravitational law can be made by setting up masses at various distances and measuring the actual force. These results can then be compared with the predictions made by the formula. The actual results can then be shown to be consistent or inconsistent with the model. A model of a system-to-be-built should also be predictive. As in the scientific case, this predictive capability will not be complete and will be qualified in various ways. Nevertheless, there are two ways in which the model must match the proposed system.

First, the behavior of an actual system built from the model must be demonstrable as being either consistent or inconsistent with the model. A model that is ambiguous or that describes a system in generalities will therefore fail in terms of rigor of representation. More to the point, a modeling language must have the means to construct a representation that can be used to evaluate objectively the actual behavior of a system. Second, the modeling language must be capable of being used to investigate the behavior of a system not yet built. This use of the system model is closer to the typical engineering use of a scale model (for example, a scale model of an airplane subjected to wind-tunnel testing) than to the scientific case. However, there is still a parallel. A scientific model, known to be consistent with certain experimental data, is often used to predict not-yet-observed behavior. Of course in the scientific case, the next step is to *measure* a *real* system to *verify* the actual behavior, and to change the model if the behavior doesn't *match*. On the other hand, in the engineering use of a system model, the next step is to *simulate* an *imaginary* system to evaluate the *predicted* behavior and to change the model if the behavior is judged *unsatisfactory*.

In addition to capability for predicting, system models should have internal characteristics that permit a choice to be made among several equivalent models. Again, there is an analogy to the scientific case. It sometimes happens that more than one model is consistent with all accessible experimental results. In this case, a choice can be made based on the principle called "Ockham's razor". In essence this states that the sparest, most economical model is the best one. (In a mathematical context this quality of a model is often called "elegance.") Ockham's razor is also applicable to system models. A systems-modeling language must therefore have internal standards by which to judge "elegance" in cases when a proposed system can be modeled in more than one way.

The preceding four sections have focused on the characteristics of the modeling language. It's now time to turn our attention to the various aspects of a real-time system that must be illuminated by the model.

3.7 Breaking the Von Neumann mind-set

A potential problem with using the flowchart as a systems-modeling notation was described in section 3.4, *Simplicity versus adequacy,* as the lack of sufficient features to express all significant aspects of systems. Following the natural-language analogy in section 3.1, one may ask about the perceptual influences of "flowchart thinking" as well as about the limitations of the flowchart notation. Actually, the limitations of our perceptions of systems can be traced beyond the flowchart to the nature of our implementation technology.

Nearly all digital processors built prior to the 1970's embody an architecture proposed by John Von Neumann [3]. These processors operate by carrying out a sequence of operations one at a time on elemental data items. The existence of this technology has served as a powerful symbol and has conditioned our perceptions accordingly. For those of us nurtured in traditional data processing environments, it is all too easy to see a problem solely in terms of sequences and of operations to be performed; that is, in terms of the *Von Neumann* mind set.

To see the limitations of sequential perception, imagine the task of adding the magnitudes of two three-dimensional vectors with identical directions. One could express this job as adding the x components of the vectors, then adding the y components, then adding the z components. The order of addition is, of course, irrelevant. However, a processor with a Von Neumann architecture must necessarily execute the addition in *some* order. It is important to be able to see this problem in terms of parallelism (possibility of concurrency) to perceive the potential for simultaneous addition of the three components. This perception is clearly important in terms of identifying potential implementations, since there are now automated array processors capable of performing such parallel computations concurrently. It is also important because regardless of the implementation, certain problems (for example, simultaneous monitoring of continuous variables) are easier to think about in terms of parallelism.

In addition to the limitations of sequential perception, there are also limits imposed by perceiving things strictly in terms of operations. For example, consider the problem of displaying a list in numerical order on demand. The problem can be thought of as a more complex operation (ordering followed by displaying) performed on a collection of unorganized data (the list elements) or as a simpler operation (displaying) performed on an organized data object (the ordered list). In moving from the first perception to the second, some of the "weight" of the problem has been transferred from the active, operational sphere to the passive, structural sphere. This is important not only for more efficient implementations, when simpler operations may mean faster response, but also for a more flexible conceptualization of systems.

In creating a systems-modeling language, then, it is vital to provide a notation that facilitates a conception of the problem with minimal artificial restrictions. The language must be capable of formulating problems and expressing solutions in terms of parallelism and data structures as well as in terms of sequence and operations.

3.8 Modeling data and control

In discussing the Von Neumann mind-set in the last section, we looked at the list to be printed from a static point of view, in terms of the presence or absence of internal structure. It is also possible for us to look at data from the point of view of its availability to a processor and to ask whether a system can perform some work that requires a particular piece of data as input.

From a processing perspective, there are two distinct issues relating to a process: the availability of the data necessary for the performance of the process and the occurrence of the environmental conditions sufficient for the process. There is a potential for confusion between these issues because there exists a large class of systems in which the availability of the data is the sufficient condition. From a requirements-definition view-point, many typical business systems are transaction driven. An inventory management system records an increase in on-hand balance, for instance, whenever an inventory item identification and quantity added "arrive." The requirements-definition strategies of Ross [4], Gane and Sarson [5], and DeMarco [6] take advantage of this characteristic by using a "data flow" modeling notation. Input data is pictured as entering a process, that is thereby triggered to produce an output that may then enter another process, and so on.

A modeling language that is to be adequate for real-time systems must be capable of separating the *data* needed by a process from the *control* that actually makes the process operate. Consider, for example, the position of a variable-flow valve that is input data for a process-control system. The data is always available. However, a process that uses the valve position may operate only during time intervals when the tank is being filled, intervals determined by environmental conditions. The process will not be triggered simply by the data's availability. An adequate systems modeling language must therefore allow modeling of control as well as data.

3.9 Modeling continuity and discontinuity

The distinction between continuous and discontinuous behavior is of immense significance in a wide variety of disciplines. Take physics as an example; one of the major breakthroughs of the last hundred years was the discovery that electrons, rather than being free to occupy any position around a nucleus, are restricted to discrete, quantized orbits. The major systems modeling issue in which continuity versus discontinuity is a factor is the behavior of a system over time.

Let's consider the status of inputs and outputs as related to the "real-time" of a system. In other words, if one watched the inputs and outputs of a system as it operated, what would one see? Take the instance of an analog circuit that monitors a signal from a thermocouple and produces a variable-voltage output signal that controls the power supplied to a heating coil. The inputs and outputs in this case are *time-continuous*. They have signifcant values at every point over the time intervals when the control loop is active. On the other hand, a system that monitors the impact of particles on a detector in a high-energy physics experiment can be said to have input data that is *time-discrete*, which exists only at isolated points in time.

In most real-time systems there is a complex interplay between time-continuous and time-discrete behavior. The temperature control circuit just mentioned, if activated and deactivated by an on-off switch, exhibits two different kinds of time-continuous behavior. During periods after an "off" and before an "on," its output is null for any value of the input. During periods after an "on" and before an "off", its output is related to its input by the algorithm imbedded in its control circuitry. The time-discrete events of the "on" and "off" signals cause transitions between one kind of behavior and the other.

The distinction between time-continuous and time-discrete behavior is closely related to the distinction between data and control. In the temperature-control analog circuit, the temperature is the data and the on-off switch is the control. However, the data/contol perspective is not the same as the continuous/discrete perspective. The heater control output would often be referred to as a "control signal," yet is time-continuous in nature. On the other hand, the pulse indicating that a particle has hit the detector in the physics experiment could well be considered "data."

In order to model the time-related complexities of a real-time system, an adequate modeling language must be able to distinguish time-continuous and time-discrete behaviors and must be able to model the interactions between the two.

3.10 Summary

Building a model of a complex system to be developed is too complex and error-prone a task to be approached without a careful consideration of the modeling language to be used. The choice of specific notations, modeling disciplines, and technical methodologies can either greatly help or greatly hinder the systems development process. The systems development approach we shall describe in the Tools sections of this book, was carefully constructed to make the best possible use of models in the systems development environment.

Chapter 3: References

1. M. McLuhan and Q. Fiore, *The Medium Is the Message*. New York: Bantam Books, 1967.

2. R. Block. *The Politics of Projects*. New York: Yourdon Press, 1983.

3. J. Von Neumann. First Draft of a Report on the EDVAC. Philadelphia, 1945.

4. D.T. Ross and K.E. Schoman, Jr. "Structured Analysis for Requirements Definition." *IEEE Transactions on Software Engineering* (January 1977), Vol.SE-3, No. 5, pp.6-15

5. C. Gane and T. Sarson, "Structured Systems Analysis: Tools & Techniques." Improved System Technologies, New York: 1977.

6. T. DeMarco. *Structured Analysis and System Specification*. New York: Yourdon Press, 1978, pp.314-15.

4
Modeling Heuristics

4.1 Introduction

In Chapter 3 we argued that a good modeling tool reduces the conceptual distance between the developer's mental representation of a problem and the external representation needed for implementation. One of the examples we gave was the FORTRAN language. Since most people with science or engineering training learn to think in terms of manipulation of algebraic variables, FORTRAN allows a straightforward way to translate these thoughts about computations into usable form. In the ideal case one can picture the process as simply "transcribing" a mental representation into FORTRAN via a display terminal keyboard.

A modeling language having all the characteristics outlined in Chapter 3 should be more convenient than FORTRAN for representing a class of system that goes beyond sequences of variable manipulations. Is it then possible that a developer can learn to think in terms of this broader language? Is it also possible that building a real-time system model can be reduced to a transcription process? While the answer to the first question is yes, the answer to the second is a very definite no. The problem concerns not the modeling language, but the intrinsic limitations of human mental processes — limitations that apply to FORTRAN-style variable-manipulation problems as well as to more general systems. Human beings are generally not capable of holding all the details of a problem in their minds once the problem exceeds a modest degree of complexity. This limitation manifests itself in the form of "fuzziness" in the understanding of a system. A developer may understand the overall layout of a system well but may be fuzzy about the details. Conversely, the developer may understand various elements of a system in detail but may be fuzzy about how the details fit together.

It is therefore desirable to give the model builder more than an adequate notation to facilitate the system-building process. These additional aids take the form of *modeling heuristics* — approaches with a reasonable history of success but with no guarantees.

4.2 Nature of modeling heuristics

Heuristics cannot be proven to work in the same sense as a notation can be proven to be adequate for representing a class of problems. Nevertheless, the application of a heuristic often succeeds in translating a fuzzy concept into the more precise representation of some modeling notation. Most modeling heuristics are applications of the general principle that Weinberg [1] has formulated as the *Lump Law:* "In order to understand anything, you musn't try to understand everything." Heuristics provide guidelines for differentiating aspects of a problem; the model builder "lumps" certain elements of a system together so they can be dealt with separately.

A widely applied heuristic is that of "top-down" development. The modeler writes a brief description of a problem to be solved (in this case, a system to be characterized) and then attempts to divide the problem into a mutually exclusive set of sub-problems that together are equivalent to the original problem. Each sub-problem is then divided into a set of sub-sub-problems, and the process is repeated recursively until the lowest level of descriptions is small enough for the modeler's purpose. Take an example drawn from chemical engineering. The problem of producing a product from reactants may be divided into the following three sub-problems: getting the reactants into a reaction vessel, carrying out the reaction, and getting the product out of the reation vessel. The first subproblem may be divided into a sub-sub-problem for each reactant to be put into the vessel, and the process may be continued in a similar fashion. At each level of the process, the sub-problems not being worked on are conveniently "lumped" for deferred consideration. For instance, the details of performing the reaction can be ignored when considering getting the reactants into the vessel.

Another heuristic, proposed by Orr [2], is working backwards from the required outputs of a system. The modeler imagines the output as being the result of an assembly-line process and asks, What are the major components from which the output can be assembled? Each component is then subjected to the same process until the "earliest" set of components can be identified with pieces of available inputs. The process is very similar in nature to "top-down" development; it might be called "output-backwards" development.

4.3 Varieties of heuristics

The two heuristics described in the preceding section are both very general in nature and could be used in conjunction with virtually any modeling notation. There are heuristics, however, whose application depends on specific capabilities of a modeling notation. As an illustration, let's look at a problem in the application of top-down development. Very often there are a variety of ways that a system can be divided into sub-systems. How is a modeler to choose among a set of possible decompositions? A criterion suggested by DeMarco [3] in conjunction with the data flow approach to requirements definition is "Partition to minimize interfaces"; that is, the decomposition that results in the minimum number of connections among subsystems is the best one. However, to apply this guideline effectively in a complex situation, it must be possible to represent the interconnections between subsystems in some modeling notation.

One can also turn this idea around. A notation that permits the modeler to describe interfaces among subsystems is of much more use when coupled with guidelines for choosing among a set of possible interfaces.

As mentioned in the preface, we and our colleagues have had extensive opportunities to observe and assist systems developers at work in a variety of situations. The heuristics presented in this book are a distillation and refinement of what has been seen to work well — an attempt to bring to consciousness the often elusive thought process by which a vague conception becomes a precise description of some desired aspect of a system. In the following chapters, a wide variety of modeling heuristics will be presented. Some are quite specific to a particular notation, allowing the evaluation of a model's ability to communicate effectively. These will be presented as *semantic clarity rules.* Other heuristics assist in deciding how to represent some feature of the real world in a model. For instance, we will present guidelines for deciding whether to represent aspects of a system's environment in time-continuous or time-discrete terms.

In the remaining sections of this chapter, we will present two heuristics of such general importance that they color our entire approach to systems development: separation of essence from implementation and organizing for independence.

4.4 Separating essence from implementation

The systems development process has often been divided to reflect the traditional human distinction between "the problem" and "the solution." Separating systems analysis from systems design, and distinguishing functional specifications, system designs, and program designs as project deliverables are methods used to organize the work of development around this separation. The fact that analysis and design are often not separated in practice and the frequent lack of agreement over whether some detail relates to requirements definition or to design are signs that the division has not worked as well as could be hoped.

DeMarco [4] and others have attempted to emphasize this division by distinguishing *logical* from *physical* system models. A significant refinement relating to problem/solution separation has been developed by McMenamin and Palmer [5]. The overall structure of the modeling strategy used in this book is based on their work and involves separating the *essence* of a system from its *implementation*. (McMenamin and Palmer use the word *incarnation* instead of *implementation.)* Given that a system must function in a specific environment and given that it has a purpose to accomplish, it is possible to describe what it must do (the *essential activities)* and what data it must store (the *essential memory)* so that the description is true regardless of the technology used to implement the system. Such a description is called an *essential model.*

We'll use as an example an embedded system that controls the movement of liquid in and out of a reaction vessel. In order to fulfill its purpose, the system must do the following: Respond to something in the environment that indicates the reaction is ready to go by opening an input valve. Respond to the desired level of liquid being present in the vessel by closing the input valve. Respond to something in the environment that indicates the reaction is completed by opening an output valve. Respond to the liquid being completely removed from the tank by closing the output valve.

This description must be satisfied by any system serving this purpose in this environment, whether the system as implemented consists of analog circuitry, instructions executed by a digital computer with analog-to-digital and digital-to-analog peripherals, or a human being manually opening or closing the valves. The idea of an essential model relates to the thought process used to select the content of the model, not to the modeling notation; notice that the essential model just presented was in narrative form.

It is also possible to describe a system as actually realized by a particular technology. A model incorporating such description is called an *implementation model.* In the case of the system just described, a particular implementation model might state: The sensing of conditions and the opening and closing of valves is controlled by a task executing under a multi-tasking operating system on a microprocessor. The level of the tank is indicated by a voltage on an analog input line with a range of $+6$ to -6 volts, with the high voltage indicating an overflow and the low voltage indicating empty. The positions of the input and output valves are set by 16-bit words placed in digital-to-analog buffer registers and used to set output voltages, with a word of ones representing complete opening of the valve and a word of zeros representing complete closing.

Implementation details of the type just given are not sufficient to permit a system builder to create a working system unless the builder also has access to the content of the essential model. The implementation model is defined as an elaboration of the essential model that contains enough detail to permit a successful implementation with a particular technology.

A major benefit of the essential-model/implementation-model approach lies in its resolution of a classic confusion between *implementation dependence* and *level of detail*. Developers commonly regard high-level details of a system as belonging to requirements definition (the problem) and low-level details as belonging to design (the solution). In the approach described here, details at all levels can relate either to the problem or to the solution. The embedded flow-control system described a few paragraphs earlier might need to fill the vessel to a depth of $3.752 \pm .004$ meters. This is certainly a detail; one can understand the requirements in considerable depth without knowing this fact. However, the required depth of filling and the associated tolerance is not technology-dependent. Any processor performing the filling would have to honor this constraint, which depends on the nature of the environment and thus belongs to the essential model. The fact that the system will utilize a microprocessor rather than analog-control circuitry, on the other hand, is a very high-level issue, but one that belongs in the implementation model rather than in the essential model. Figure 4.1 illustrates the relationship between the two models.

The spiral arrow in Figure 4.1 also suggests another feature of the essential/implementation distinction, namely that the sequence of construction is independent of model content. While it is certainly possible to complete the essential model before beginning the implementation model, it is also possible to proceed as in Figure 4.1. Here the high-level essential details are determined, the corresponding details of an implementation are filled in, the next lower level of essential detail is created, and so on. The procedure for building the two models is really a project management issue. The heuristic only requires that the thought processes involved in essential and implementation modeling, and the resultant models themselves, be separate.

There are a number of major benefits to be gained from the separation of the essential model from the implementation model. First, the essential model is expressed in terms of the subject-matter vocabulary of the system. An avionics simulator, for example, would be described in terms of flight instrument readings, pilot commands, and control surfaces, rather than in terms of computer hardware or software technology. This feature of the essential model should facilitate review and verification of the model by subject-matter experts. It should also minimize bias by omitting implementation details that might force favoring one technology over another. Second, since any complete implementation model must contain all essential-model details, the finished essential model is by definition the smallest complete model of a system that can be built. Since the ease of review of a model is a non-linear function of its size, the essential-modeling strategy should maximize the probability of requirements-definition errors being caught during model review. Finally, the separation of the essential and implementation models permits them to be compared for consistency. The implementation model is a mapping of the essential model onto a technological environment; therefore a correct implementation model must preserve the behavior described by the essential model, and a failure to preserve this behavior must be resolved by repairing the implementation model. Once consistency of the two models has been established, it should be possible to trace a particular aspect of the problem forward to its implementation or to trace a particular implementation detail back to the requirement that motivated it.

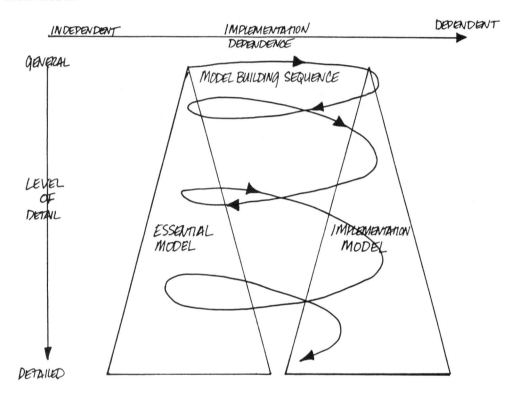

Figure 4.1. Relationship of essential and implementation models.

Further details about the distinction between the two types of models, and practical guidelines for making the distinction, will be presented in later chapters. Now let's explore the other general-purpose heuristic that permeates our systems development approach.

4.5 Organizing for maximum independence

There is an underlying principle of systems development, expressed in various ways, that equates good organization with independence of parts. A good model and a good implementation will keep related things together and unrelated things apart.

As an example, let's examine a system that monitors a number of external devices. Errors detected in the operation of the devices are to be logged to a common error list, which is printed in its entirety at periodic intervals. One organization would embed in each piece of the system that monitors a device a sequence of instructions something like

```
if (error and e <emax) then
    e=e+1
    errorlist(e) =currenterror
else
    signal (errorlistoverflow)
```

In addition, the code that printed the error list would need to contain

```
for i from 1 to e
    printline = errorlist(i)
    -
    -
    -
    -
e=0
```

Although the organization of the error list is quite simple, if the system monitors N devices there are $N+1$ points in the code that must "know" how many errors are currently in the list, $N+1$ points which must "know" that the list makes use of the array-handling capabilities of the programming language, and N points that must "know" the storage limit of the list.

As an alternative, consider placing in each piece of code that monitors a device an invocation of

> if error then
>   puterror (currenterror, overflow)

where *overflow* is a flag set true or false by the invoked routine. The print routine would now contain

```
initgeterror
until ( endlist )
 geterror(printline,endlist)
 -

 -

 -
```

To complete the organization, a utility routine would be created as follows:

```
puterror (x,y)
 if e < emax then
  e=e+1
  errorlist (e)=x
  y=false
 else
  y=true

initgeterror
 i=0
 return

geterror (x,y)
 if i<e then
  i=i+1
  x=errorlist (i)
  y=false
 else
  y=true
  e=0
```

The data items *e, emax,* and *i,* and the use of the array to store the list, are completely local to the utility routine; the mechanism for maintaining the list is completely hidden from the rest of the application code. Moving the list from an array to an external file or ordering the list as it is being created can be accomplished strictly within the confines of the utility routine. The mechanism is totally independent of the use of the error list.

This code-oriented example is based on the principles advocated by Parnas [6] in the context of software module design under the name of *information hiding.* However, this is but one expression of the same general principle: organize for maximum independence. DeMarco [7] expressed this theme as "Partition to minimize interfaces." Weinberg [8] refers to *encapsulation* — the idea that the details of a function can be hidden from others. Stevens, Myers, and Constantine [9] developed the twin ideas of cohesion (the measure of relatedness of elements within a module) and coupling (the measure of interconnectedness between modules). While each of these ideas focuses on different parts of the development process, the same heuristic is being applied.

4.6 Summary

Building a model of a system is a complex task that requires good judgment; it is not a mechanical exercise. Our judgment can be guided by rules-of-thumb or heuristics that provide us with general principles for model construction. We have introduced two of these principles: separating essential from implementation and organizing for maximum independence. As we develop techniques for the construction of the models, we shall see these principles in use repeatedly.

Chapter 4: References

1. G. Weinberg, *An Introduction to General Systems Thinking.* New York: John Wiley & Sons, 1975.

2. K. Orr, *Structured Requirements Definition.* Topeka: Ken Orr and Associates, 1983.

3. T. DeMarco, *Structured Analysis and System Specification.* New York: Yourdon Press, 1978.

4. T. DeMarco, op. cit.

5. S. McMenamin and J. Palmer, *Essential Systems Analysis.* New York: Yourdon Press, 1984.

6. D. Parnas. "On the Criteria to Be Used in Decomposing Systems into Modules." *Communications of the ACM,* Vol. 5, No. 12 (December 1972), pp. 1053-58.

7. T. DeMarco. op. cit.

8. G. Weinberg. op. cit.

9. W. Stevens, G. Myers, and L. Constantine. "Structured Design" *IBM Systems Journal,* Vol. 13, No. 2 (May 1974), pp. 115-39.

5
The Modeling Process

In Chapter 3 we introduced the idea of using a modeling language as a step in the systems development process. We suggested that, instead of rushing immediately into implementation, developers will find it more effective to model what is intended first, review and modify the model extensively, and then use the model as a plan for implementation. In this way, we can change the giant step of proceeding from a bright idea to a running system into several smaller steps, each checkpointed by a reviewed model.

The steps that developers choose to make on the way to a running system constitute a *systems development life cycle*, and each step in the life cycle is represented by a visible reviewable *model*. Each systems development project has a different set of technical problems, and, even when two projects share a common problem, the respective sizes of that problem can differ widely. Each project must therefore choose the steps that make up the life cycle for that project, and that project only. In addition, each model must be expressed by some notation, preferably one with the desirable characteristics outlined in Chapter 3. Please note that the the life cycle is defined by the steps chosen, and not by the notation used. It is the task of the technical project manager to define the intent and form of each step[1].

The systems we characterized as real-time in Chapter 2 can require very different life cycles. Nevertheless, there are some general principles that apply to any life cycle. These are the following: Each successive model is derived from the previous model by incorporating additional information that was suppressed or ignored in the previous model. The information that we choose to suppress for a given model should have a low risk of coming back to surprise us later.

In addition to the general principles, there also are types of models that will appear in most life cycles. In Chapter 4, we made a major distinction between two forms of model: an essential model, which is an implementation-free statement of what needs to be done, and an implementation model, which states how technology will be used to carry out the essential-model functions. This separation adheres to our principles in that we derive the implementation model from the essential model by adding information about the implementation technology. Also, there is a low risk of being surprised by the decisions about the implementation technology, as long as we remember that real-time systems may be close to the threshold of what our technology can do, and we have a reasonable chance of being able to acquire the kind of processing power we require. From these two models we should be able to proceed with reasonable confidence into the construction of the system. This basic plan of attack is outlined in Table 5.1.

For most complex systems, however, some further distinctions are useful. We have chosen to break down the models into more stages, which are described below.

Activity	Comment
build essential model	describe required behavior of system
build implementation model	describe automated technology organization that embodies required behavior
build system	embody implementation model in hardware and software

Direction of Evolution

Table 5.1. Evolution of a system.

5.1 The essential model

The essential model consists of two parts: a model which focuses on defining what the system must interact with, and a model which describes the required behavior of the system. Both models are implementation-free; that is, there are no assumptions made about the technology to be used to implement the system. Both models, however, must account for the implementation technology used in the environment (which, by definition, is not a part of the system), including those issues associated with faults or errors.

The Environmental Model is a description of the environment in which the system operates. This model has two pieces: a description of the boundary between the system and the environment, showing the interfaces between the two parts, and a description of the events that occur in the environment to which the system must respond. *The Behavioral Model* is a description of the required behavior of the system. This model also has two pieces that are connected: the transformation schema and the data schema with their associated specifics. The transformation schema denotes graphically the layout of the transformations that operate on flows that cross the system boundary, and it is the active portion of the system that responds to events that occur in the environment. The data schema denotes graphically the layout of information that must be remembered by the system for it to operate. This organization of the models is described in Table 5.2.

ENVIRONMENTAL MODEL	DESCRIPTION OF THE ENVIRONMENT IN WHICH THE SYSTEM OPERATES	CONTEXT DIAGRAM	DESCRIPTION OF THE BOUNDARY THAT SEPARATES THE SYSTEM FROM ITS ENVIRONMENT
		EVENT LIST	DESCRIPTION OF EXTERNAL EVENTS IN THE ENVIRONMENT TO WHICH THE SYSTEM MUST RESPOND
BEHAVIORAL MODEL	DESCRIPTION OF BEHAVIOR IN RESPONSE TO EVENTS IN ENVIRONMENT	TRANSFORMATION SCHEMA AND SPECIFICS	DESCRIPTION OF THE TRANSFORMATIONS THE SYSTEM MAKES IN RESPONSE TO EVENTS
		DATA SCHEMA AND SPECIFICS	DESCRIPTION OF THE INFORMATION THE SYSTEM MUST HAVE IN ORDER TO RESPOND

Table 5.2. Essential model layout.

5.2 The implementation models

The task of adding in the implementation technology for a real-time system can be long and complex. We introduce the implementation technology in a series of steps, differentiating between the different aspects in terms of the concurrency characteristics of the technology. (Table 5.3.)

The first level is the introduction of processors to carry out the activities and store the data declared by the essential model. We think of each processor as being truly concurrent with other processors. Next, we must introduce the technology within processors: namely, tasks, or chunks of code that can be scheduled as a unit; and the named storage units that they share. Within a single processor, processes *simulate* concurrency.

PROCESSOR	DESCRIPTION OF THE CHOSEN ALLOCATION TO PROCESSORS, AND THEIR INTERFACE	TRANSFORMATION AND DATA SCHEMAS WITH THEIR SPECIFICS	DESCRIPTION OF THE TRANSFORMATIONS AND STORED DATA ALLOCATED TO PROCESSORS AND TASKS, AND THEIR INTERFACES
TASK	DESCRIPTION OF THE CHOSEN ALLOCATION TO TASKS AND THEIR INTERFACES		
MODULE	DESCRIPTION OF THE CHOSEN ALLOCATION TO MODULES, AND THEIR INTERFACES	STRUCTURE CHARTS AND THEIR SPECIFICS	DESCRIPTION OF THE HIERARCHICAL ORGANIZATION OF MODULES IN A PROGRAM

Table 5.3   Implementation model layout.

Finally, we must introduce the technology of module organization, usually defined by a programming language. Here we assume that there is no concurrency; modules are called, and when their task is complete, they return to their caller, who is waiting for their completion. Some of today's programming languages, such as Ada, provide facilities for asynchronous calls, which we shall model at the task level.

The Processor Model shows the decisions we make about processors and the interfaces between them. Each processor is responsible for some portion of the essential model. *The Task Model* shows the decisions we make about tasks and the interfaces between them. Different processors have different internal software organizations, which we shall refer to as a *software architecture*. The model must show this internal organization if some portions of the essential model are carried out by this software system. *The Module Model* shows the decisions we make about the allocation of essential model activities to modules, and the interfaces between them within a single task.

We will continue to use the transformation and data schemas to model the introduction of processors and tasks, since both permit concurrent processing, fow which the transformation schema is designed. The module model will be illuminated using another tool, the *structure chart,* which uses a different notation to illuminate synchronous calls.

5.3 A real-time systems development methodology?

We must emphasize that the models we have laid out above do not constitute a development methodology for a project. Each project must tune, or tailor, this general scheme for its own use. Consider, for example, a system that is implemented on a single processor; there is little use in constructing a model of the allocation at the processor level, since this would simply be a redrawing, showing very little additional information.

The models we shall be describing, however, do represent a general scheme for proceeding with real-time systems development. As we describe each model in detail, we shall identify and characterize the information being added at each step.

5.4 Organization of topics

As pointed out in the preceding two chapters, we distinguish between modeling languages and modeling heuristics. The material on modeling languages describes various modeling notations, while the material on modeling heuristics focuses on the application of the notations to common modeling situations. We have used this distinction to organize our presentation of the material in the three volumes planned for this book, of which this is the first. The organization is as follows: The Tools section introduces an integrated collection of tools that can be applied equally well to the building of either an essential model or the highest levels of an implementation model (Vol. 1). The Essential Modeling Heuristics section provides guidelines for using the generalized modeling tools to build an Essential Model (Vol.2). The Processor and Task Stage Heuristics section provides guidelines for using the generalized modeling tools to map the Essential Model into Processor and Task Models (Vol 3.). The Module Stage Tools and Heuristics section introduces a specialized notation for the description of code organization and provides guidelines for mapping of the systems-level implementation model into the Module Model (Vol 3).

5.5 Summary

The combination of a set of modeling tools and a set of guidelines for applying these tools permits the construction of a life cycle for a particular project. The life cycle plan specifies a sequence of models that are the deliverables of the project. The organization of topics in this book has been chosen to facilitate the selection of a project life cycle, based on a generally applicable sequence of models and a generally useful set of tools.

Chapter 5: References

1.   Sally Shlaer, Diana Grand, and Stephen Mellor. "The Project Matrix: A Model for Software Engineering Management." *Proceedings of the Third IEEE Software Engineering Standards Applications Workshop*, October 1984.

SECTION 2
TOOLS

Section 2 describes a set of modeling tools comprehensive enough to model real-time systems.

The figure below describes the overall layout of the section.

Chapters 6 through 9 introduce tools for modeling transformations — the active part of a system. Chapter 6 introduces the transformations and the connections between them. Chapter 7 describes a set of graphic tools for specifying the details of control transformations, thus providing a description of the dynamic behavior of the system. Chapter 8 provides a set of corrresponding tools for specifying data transformations. Finally, Chapter 9 focuses on the execution of the transformation schema; it supplies tools for checking the rigor of the specification.

Chapter 10 introduces a graphic tool for modeling the organization of stored data — the passive part of a system. The data schema declares categories of stored data and the relationships between them. We use this model in a restricted sense, focusing only on the data stored within a particular system. Chapter 11 describes tools for specifying the meaning, composition, and type of data, whether that data is derived from the transformation schema or the data schema.

Chapter 12 describes a scheme for organizing the models for easy presentation and verification.

Finally, Chapter 13 defines rules for checking that the components of the model are consistent with each other. This provides for an integrated set of models: The two schemas are integrated and so are the models produced as summaries and their more detailed representations.

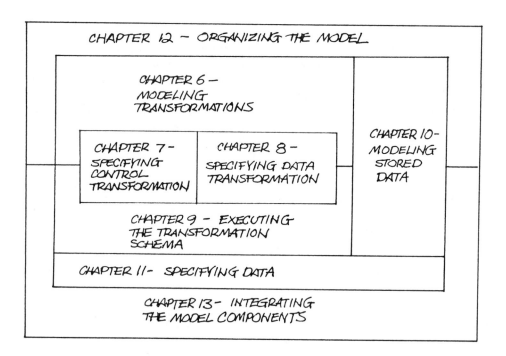

CHAPTER 12 — ORGANIZING THE MODEL

CHAPTER 6 —
MODELING
TRANSFORMATIONS

CHAPTER 7 —
SPECIFYING
CONTROL
TRANSFORMATION

CHAPTER 8 —
SPECIFYING DATA
TRANSFORMATION

CHAPTER 10 —
MODELING
STORED
DATA

CHAPTER 9 — EXECUTING
THE TRANSFORMATION
SCHEMA

CHAPTER 11 — SPECIFYING DATA

CHAPTER 13 — INTEGRATING
THE MODEL COMPONENTS

6

Modeling Transformations

6.1 Introduction

The *transformation schema* models a system as an active entity — as a network of activities that accept and produce data and control messages (and sometimes material or energy). In this chapter we will introduce the notation for the transformation schema, give some examples of its use, and describe the guidelines for assessing the consistency and the communicational quality of the model.

The transformation schema is based on the notation for data flow diagrams proposed by DeMarco [1] with substantial extensions to improve its rigor and representational ability.

6.2 The static view

Before looking at the active nature of the transformation schema, let's use it to portray some static relationships.

Consider the processing applied to an encrypted message to produce a message in plain text. The associated transformation schema is shown in Figure 6.1. The notation shows inputs and outputs as labeled arrows (*flows*) and represents the work done to produce the outputs as a labeled circle (the *transformation*.) As mentioned above, although most transformation schemas show flows or transformations of *data*, the notation can also represent *material* or *energy* flows and transformations.

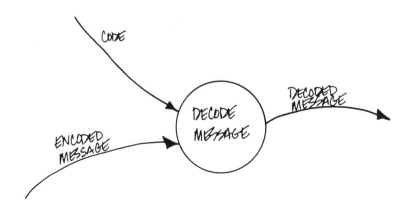

Figure 6.1. Transformation schema basic notation.

A typical schema contains not a single transformation but a set of related transformations, as in the example of Figure 6.2. In this figure there is a sequential relationship, between the transformations; the output from Encode Message is the input to Prepare Message for Transmission. The transformation schema is also capable of representing parallel transformations (Figure 6.3): Produce Terrain Map and Produce Weather Summary are completely independent of one another; they are not required to be ordered sequentially because of input/output relationships.

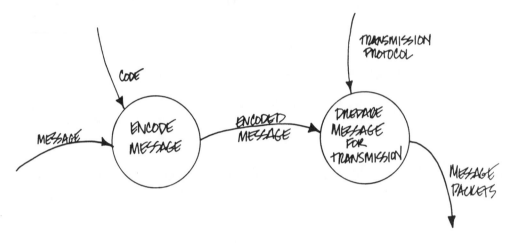

Figure 6.2.   Linked transformations.

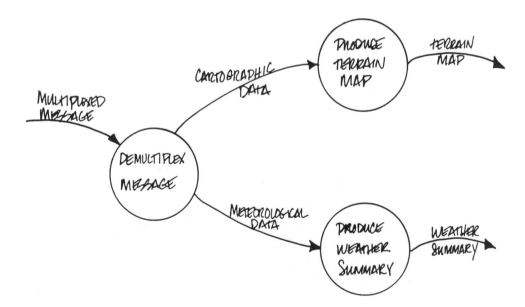

Figure 6.3.   Parallel transformations.

Separate flows (such as the output flows from two preceding transformations) may be shown converging to a single input to a succeeding transformation. Similarly, a single flow may diverge if subsets of the output flow are inputs to two or more succeeding transformations or if the entire output is used by two or more succeeding transformations (Figure 6.4).

CONVENTION	INTERPRETATION
Z → X, Y	TWO SUBSETS OF Z ARE USED BY TWO DIFFERENT SUCCESSOR TRANSFORMATIONS
Z → →	ALL OF Z IS USED BY TWO DIFFERENT SUCCESSOR TRANSFORMATIONS
X, Y → Z →	Z IS COMPOSED OF TWO SUBSETS PROVIDED BY TWO PREDECESSOR TRANSFORMATIONS
→ Z →	ALL OF Z MAY BE PROVIDED BY EITHER OF TWO PREDECESSOR TRANSFORMATIONS

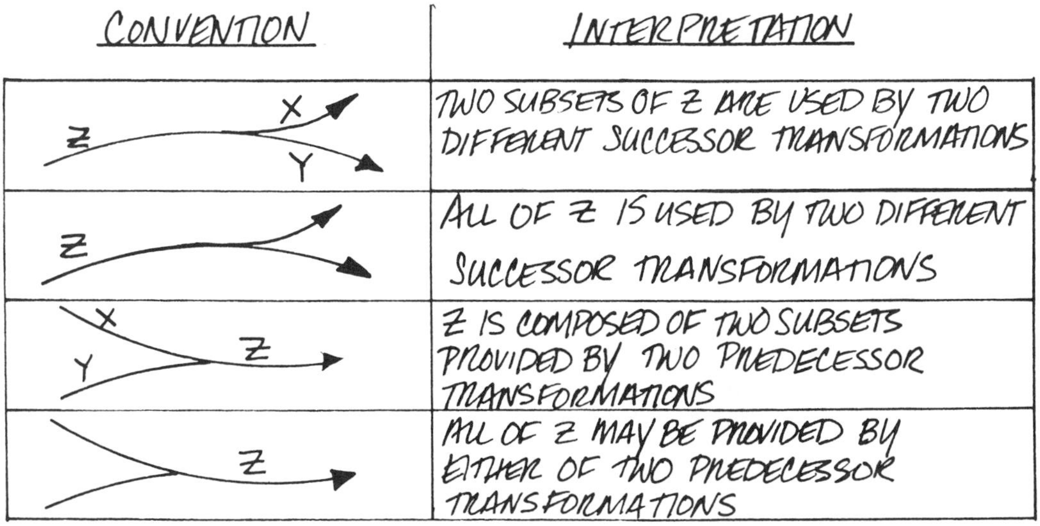

Figure 6.4. Flow convergence/divergence conventions.

Consider the set Aircraft Status with members Aircraft Number, Speed, and Altitude, and the larger set Airspace Status consisting of Aircraft Statuses for all aircraft in some airspace. Figure 6.5 shows some transformations on Airspace Status. Suppose we want to link all of them into a single transformation network. Although they are clearly related, the transformations don't have the predecessor/successor relationships that exist in Figure 6.2. Also, the labels "old" and "new" applied to Airspace Status are somewhat artificial, since the set is defined in the same way before and after the transformations are applied to it. Figure 6.6 shows the cluster of transformations operating on the Airspace Status set, which is represented as a *store*. (Although stores are typically sets, a single item that is operated on by various transformations could also be shown as a store.) The store notation is thus used to represent an item or set that is operated on by a group of transformations but whose basic character remains unchanged.

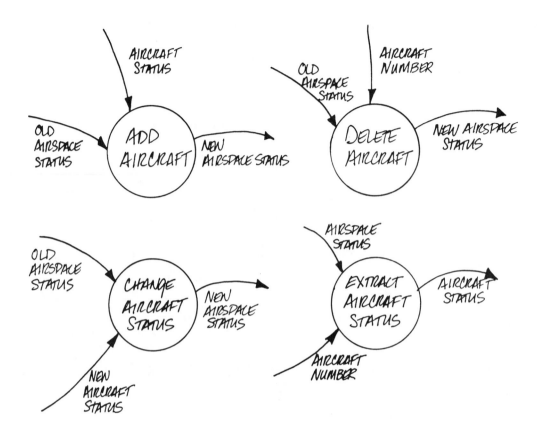

Figure 6.5. Transformations of airspace status.

The conventions for connecting transformations to stores are related to the *net flow* between them in the following ways: The flow connecting the store and the transformation is not labeled — it represents availability of the store to the transformation. An arrow head pointing from a store to a transformation means that some output flow of the transformation uses something from the store. An arrowhead pointing from a transformation to a store means that the store is changed in value(s) or in set membership by the transformation. A bi-directional arrow between a transformation and a store means that both preceding characteristics apply, and is simply a short hand for two flows — one in each direction.

Note that a flow can enter or leave a store only via a transformation. A flow that directly connects two stores, or that enters or leaves a store from outside the schema, violates the notation.

Although, the notation just presented in useful, it fails to describe a critical aspect of system behavior; this aspect will be covered in the next section.

6.3 The dynamic view

Since a system is a mechanism that operates over time, a notation that usefully represents a system will be able to describe the system's dynamic character. Let's first extend the notion of flow to include time. A *time-continuous flow*, shown with a double arrowhead, represents something that exists at every instant within a time interval, such as a variable whose value varies within some range as a continuous function of time as shown in Figure 6.7. Time-continuous flows are useful in representing characteristics of the physical environment (temperatures, voltages, and so on) that must be sensed by an embedded system and in representing output signals (for example, a desired valve position) by which an embedded system controls continuously variable aspects of outside technology. Figure 6.8 shows a transformation that adjusts the value of a time-continuous output flow in such a way as to maintain the time-continuous input flow within a value interval.

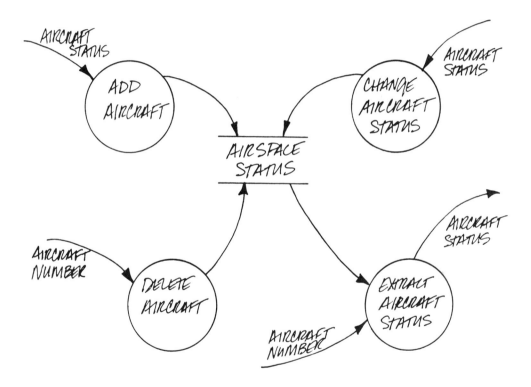

Figure 6.6. Airspace status as a store.

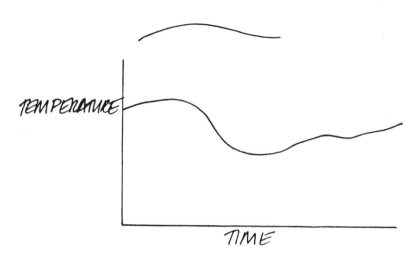

Figure 6.7. A continuous flow as a time function.

Figure 6.8. Time-continuous data flows.

In contrast to a time-continuous flow, a *time-discrete* flow, shown with a single-headed arrow, exists or has values only at individual points in time and is considered to have an undefined or null value at all other times. A time-discrete flow consisting of a set of variables is roughly equivalent to the notion of a *transaction* as used in data-processing terminology. Each point in time at which its value(s) is defined represents an *instance* of the transaction. Don't confuse the idea of a continuous time function with the notion of a continuous range of values. A variable can have a continuous range of values and still be part of a discrete flow.

Attaching time-continuous and time-discrete flows to transformations allows the behavior of the transformations to be interpreted dynamically. In Figure 6.8, for example, the transformation can be viewed as accepting input and producing output continuously over some time interval. In contrast, the transformations in Figure 6.6 accept inputs and produce outputs at discrete points in time. Continuous and discrete flows can also be combined in a single transformation. In Figure 6.9, Radar-Sensed Aircraft Position is a time-continuous input. However, its value is stored by the transformation only at the points in time when the time-discrete input Aircraft Identification Report (perhaps a radio message from the pilot) is received.

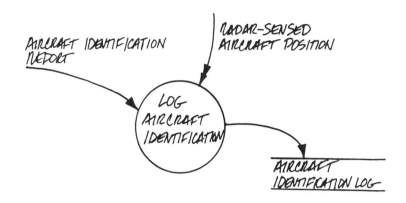

Figure 6.9. Combining time-continuous and time-discrete flows.

Finally, the concept of a store can be generalized to include the dimension of time. The items in a store remain invariant over the periods of time between the points at which transformations change them. During these time periods, the contents of the store are available to be used (incorporated into output flows) by other transformations. Referring back to Figure 6.6: if the status of a particular aircraft were placed in the Airspace Status store by Add Aircraft at time T_1, and removed by Delete Aircraft at time T_2, Extract Aircraft Status could produce the status as an output if an instance of aircraft number with a matching value occurred between T_1 and T_2; if the instance occurred before T_1 or after T_2, a null output would be produced. A store thus represents a *time-delayed* relationship between processes. Changes to, or uses of, a store are represented as occurring at discrete points in time, and thus transformation-store connections are shown as single-headed arrows.

With the dynamic interpretation, a range of complex system behaviors can be modeled with the transformation schema. However, one more extension of the notation, as described in the next section, is needed for optimum modeling power.

6.4 The event view

In the dynamic view of a system, a time-discrete data flow has two distinct characters. It represents both the *content* of the data and the *occurence* of the flow as an input or output at a specific point in time. Most real-time systems contain some flows that have *no content*, they are simply signals that indicate that something has happened or give a command. In a high-energy physics experiment, for example, a Hit flow may indicate only that a particle has hit a detector without providing any other information. In a system that controls machinery, a Start or Stop flow has the same characteristics. Such flows are called *event flows* and are represented by dotted arrows.

A transformation that accepts only event flows as inputs and produces only event flows as outputs is called a *control transformation*. It is represented as a dotted circle. Figure 6.10 shows such a transformation. Note that the transformation cannot simply pass the signals through; if a second train approaches before the first has left, the light must not be turned green upon the next Train Leaving Crossing signal.

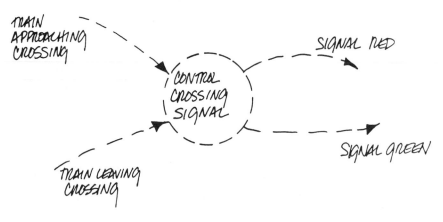

Figure 6.10. Event flows and control transformation.

We will also define an analog of a store called an *event store*. It is used to record occurrences of event flows and is represented by dotted parallel lines. In Figure 6.11, the Open Input Valve signal will not be issued in response to Start unless the Output Valve Closed signal has occurred in the interval since the last Stop signal. Note that an event flow can be connected directly to an event store with no intervening transformation. This convention is different from the one used for data stores and will be explained in the following chapter.

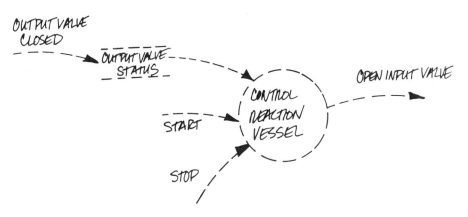

Figure 6.11. Use of an event store.

We'll provide more details about the use and interpretation of event flows, event stores, and control transformations in the next chapter. Meanwhile, the next section shows how the dynamic and event views can be superimposed.

6.5 Time-continuous vs. time-discrete behavior

Consider a system involving two quite different functions: $Y = f_1(X)$ and $Y = f_2(X)$. Y and X are time-continuous flows; at every point in time the system is accepting X as an input and producing Y as an output. The choice of the function to be used is controlled by two signals. S_1 causes the system to use f_1, and S_2 causes it to use f_2. While the system is using f_1, additional S_1 signals have no effect; the same is true of f_2 and S_2. The signals S_1 and S_2 are event flows, as defined in the last section. Figure 6.12 represents the system just described as a single transformation.

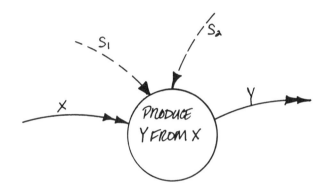

Figure 6.12. Combination of time-continuous and time-discrete behavior.

Although Figure 6.12 represents correctly the input-output relationships in the system, it conceals the details of the interplay between the time-discrete and the time-continuous behaviors. Figure 6.13, on the other hand, highlights the distinctions between the two kinds of behavior. The event flows, labeled "Enable" and "Disable," from the control transformation to the data transformations, have a special function in the model. They are to be thought of as *prompts*; they are not truly inputs to the data transformations but simply switch the data transformations on and off. The distinction between prompts and input flows is analogous to the distinction between a call to a subroutine and the parameters of a subroutine.

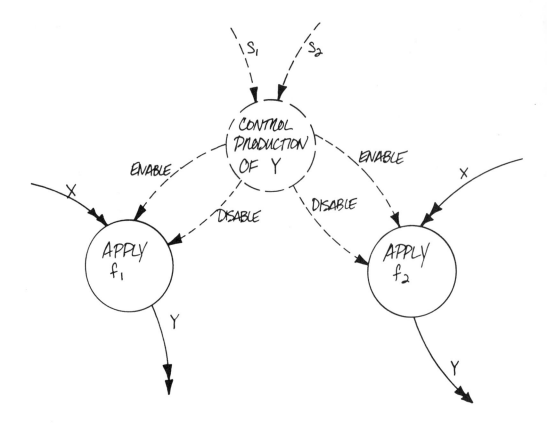

Figure 6.13. Separation of time-continuous and time-discrete behavior.

The use of event flows as prompts allows a rigorous interpretation of the behavior of data transformations over time. In Figure 6.14, Maintain Temperature produces values of Heater Control after an Enable and before a Disable, but produces no output during other time intervals. Change Aircraft Status, which has a time-discrete input flow rather than a time-continuous one, will accept Aircraft Status inputs after an Enable and before a Disable and will not accept inputs during other intervals. Finally, Record Temperature Value will place in the store the instantaneous values of Temperature at the points in time when it receives Trigger event flows. Note that there is no requirement that a data transformation be prompted. An unprompted transformation behaves the same way at all points in time.

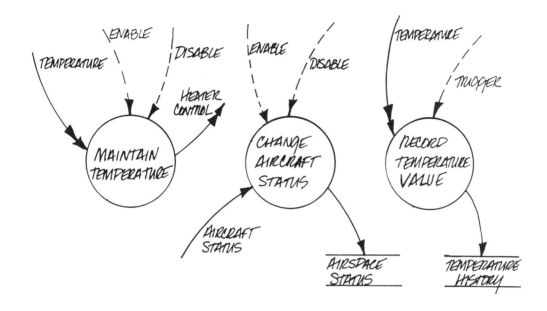

Figure 6.14. Prompted data transformations.

A modeler can rigorously separate the time-continuous and time-discrete aspects of a system if the following simple set of conventions about flows is observed: For a control transformation, only event flows are allowed as inputs and outputs. For a data transformation, only data flows are allowed as inputs, but either data flows or event flows may be produced as outputs. For both data and control transformations, incoming event flows labeled Enable, Disable, or Trigger are interpreted as prompts, not as inputs. Only control transformations may prompt other transformations.

These conventions, in addition to separating time-continuous and time-discrete behavior, separate the data and control aspects of the schema. Data transformations may exercise control *external* to the schema by creating output flows. However, only control transformations may prompt (activate and deactivate) transformations *within* the schema. Thus control is localized to the control transformations within a schema.

Let's apply these conventions to a more concrete example. Figure 6.15 shows two distinct continuous behaviors of a process control system. Although both transformations use the same input and output flows, the input-output relationships are quite different. Figure 6.16 combines these transformations with a third data transformation and a control transformation. The Enable and Disable event flows have been combined on single arrows to reduce graphic complexity. Figure 6.15 represents the following sequence:

1.   The Start event flow causes the control transformation to enable Change pH.

2.   The enabling causes Change pH to begin producing the Input Valve Control output.

3.   The input valve opens and the pH begins to change.

4.   When the pH reaches a specified value, Monitor pH sends the event flow pH at Desired Value to the control transformation.

5.   The control transformation disables Change pH and enables Maintain Constant pH.

6.   Change pH stops producing Input Valve Control and Maintain Constant pH begins producing it.

The conventions described in this section allow the modeler to combine the static and dynamic views of a system into a single integrated schema.

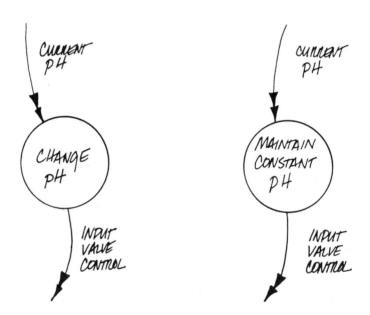

Figure 6.15. Two process-control transformations.

6.6 Multiple instances

The system modeled in Figure 6.16 may be thought of as controlling a *single* chemical reaction. We can think of the transformation schema as *declaring* the required existence of transformations used to control the reaction. However, if we now wish to model the control of *two* equivalent reactions, the dynamic aspect of the system becomes more difficult to visualize. Consider a situation in which one of the reaction vessels is maintaining a constant pH when the second reaction is started via a start event flow. What should the next output of the control transformation be? Clearly, we only want to enable Change pH for one of the reactions, leaving the other reaction busily maintaining pH. We can ask similar rude questions about the data transformations: Which ones are currently active?

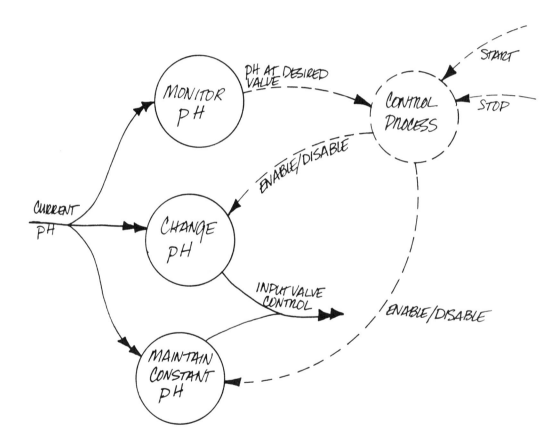

Figure 6.16. A simple process-control system.

One way out of the dilemma is to draw multiple copies of the schema, one for each reaction. This would quickly become unwieldy in a plant with a large number of equivalent reactions to be controlled. We choose instead to denote multiple instances of transformations by a double circle, used for both data and control transformations, as shown in Figure 6.17. The convention allows us to declare the required transformations once on the model, while warning the reader that multiple instantces exist.

Please note that this convention applies only to *equivalent* subsystems of a system to be developed, not to *similar* ones. Note also that the convention is useful only when some overall co-ordination of the individual instances is needed. In Figure 6.17, for example, the set of equivalent reactions may all be shut down together. If the subsystems are completely independent, it is sufficient to *model* one subsystem and to *build* multiple copies.

The remainder of this chapter is devoted to evaluation criteria for the model.

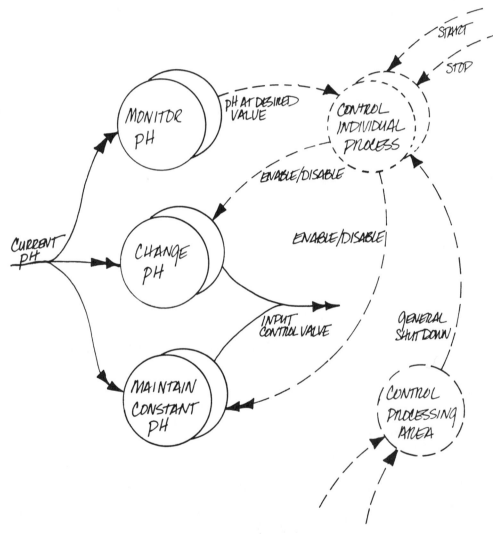

Figure 6.17. Multiple equivalent subsystems.

6.7 Correctness criteria

The modeling scheme presented in this chapter and the following chapters distributes information about a system among several modeling tools. This means that, in the broadest sense, one can only judge the correctness of the entire model, since any individual component is incomplete. Nevertheless, there are criteria that can be applied to individual components to determine correctness in a "local" sense.

The correctness criteria for the transformation schema involve determining whether the behavior of individual transformations has a reasonable interpretation. For example, the schema in Figure 6.18 has inputs, but no outputs. The transformation is a data sink; it violates the basic idea of the transformation schema as a producer of outputs from inputs. Transformations that have outputs but no inputs are also incorrect in most cases. A transformation that periodically produces a random number output or removes data from storage is an exception.

A very general principle for determining the correctness of a transformation is *conservation of data*. This simply means that the inputs to a transformation must be sufficient to produce the outputs. Figure 6.19 shows an obvious violation; the slope cannot be produced in the absence of y_2. In the case of a complex transformation, it may not be possible to determine whether data conservation is violated without knowledge of the transformation logic. However, many transformation schema errors are due to inadvertent omission of an input and may be identified by a superficial inspection.

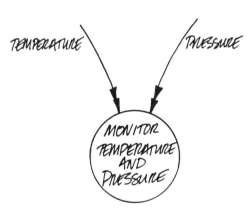

Figure 6.18. An illegal transformation.

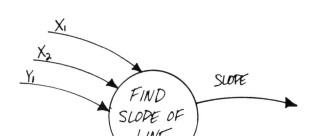

Figure 6.19. Data conservation violation.

The opposite of conservation of data may also be applied; all inputs to a transformation should be used to produce outputs. The problem in Figure 6.20 is less serious than the problem in Figure 6.19; while Figure 6.19 cannot work, Figure 6.20 merely contains a superfluous detail. Nevertheless, excess inputs should be identified and removed.

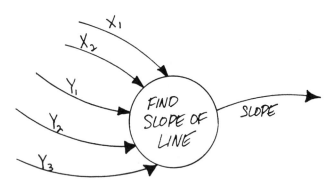

Figure 6.20. An excess input.

6.8 Interface complexity

One of the most useful features of a transformation schema is its representation of the interfaces among transformations. A glance at a data transformation to identify "busy" transformations with many inputs and outputs can give a useful impression of interface complexity. It is possible, however, to define interface complexity somewhat more formally.

A useful complexity measure for a schema is *the number of input and output tokens per transformation.* A token is an element of data that is treated as a unit by the transformation logic — one that is not decomposed into sub-elements. It is necessary to measure complexity in terms of tokens instead of flows because transformation schema conventions permit bundling of an arbitrary collection of data elements into a single flow. Both transformations in Figure 6.21 have the same complexity, since both involve five tokens.

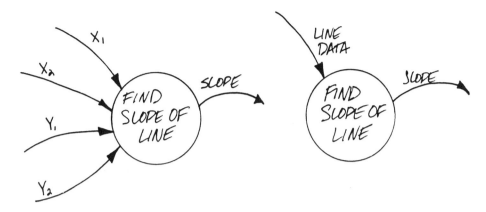

Figure 6.21. Equivalent interface complexity.

The token count, although useful, does not tell the whole story, since it focuses on the characteristics of individual transformations. It is also important to look at the complexity issue from the point of view of pairs of connected transformations. There is an important distinction between a pair of transformations connected by a flow and a pair connected through a store. On the left-hand side of Figure 6.22, there is a *causal connection* between transformations X and Y. The production of an output by X causes Y to operate, and so X and Y must be synchronized. On the right-hand side of Figure 6.22, there is no causal connection. The production of output by X has no immediate effect on Y. For the remainder of this discussion, only direct-flow connections will be used in complexity determinations.

The characteristic employment of interface complexity measurements is to compare alternatives for dividing a system into a set of transformations. Consider a system that monitors and controls three independent variables — temperature, fluid level, and pH — in a process control system. The processing of each variable involves scaling the input signal, determining the required control output, and storing the scaled input value. Figures 6.23 and 6.24 show two ways of dividing this system into three transformations. Figure 6.24 is clearly simpler in terms of interface complexity; there are *no* direct flow connections among the transformations.

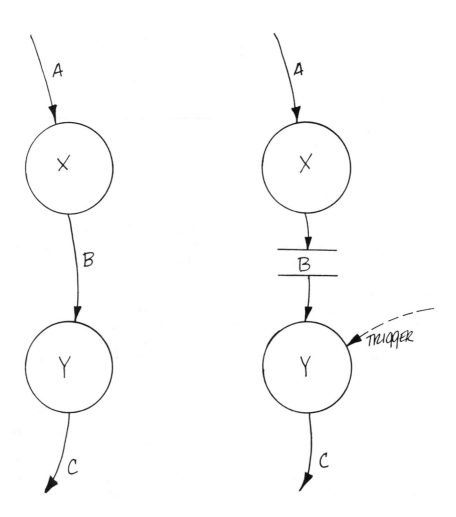

Figure 6.22. Causal and non-causal interfaces.

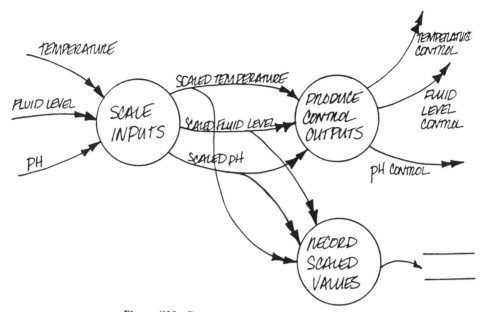

Figure 6.23. Process-control system, version 1.

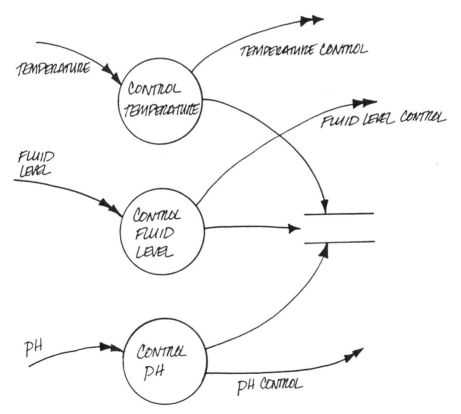

Figure 6.24. Process-control system, version 2.

6.9 Synchronous transformations

Since the transformation schema provides only a schematic view of a system, a complete understanding of a transformation requires a detailed specification of its logic. Nevertheless, as shown earlier in the chapter, many aspects of the behavior of a transformation may be deduced from the schema alone. Differentiating between time-continuous flows, time-discrete flows, and prompts allows us to say whether a transformation's behavior is continuous over time, whether it responds unconditionally at every point in time to the arrival of an input, and so on.

A transformation that has two or more discrete input data flows introduces ambiguity into this kind of time-dependent interpretation. For example, the transformation shown in Figure 6.25 allows either of two interpretations. Either two matching input flows must arrive at the same instant in time for the transformation logic to be carried out, or matching inputs may arrive at different points in time, and the logic contains an internal storage and matching mechanism.

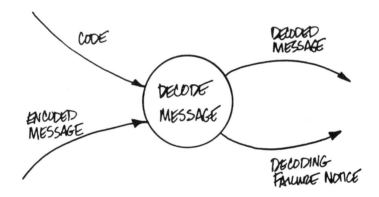

Figure 6.25. An ambiguous transformation.

Even the static interpretation of this transformation is ambiguous, since some instances of Encoded Message may allow the production of an output without the need for a Code input, if the code is incorporated into the transformation logic.

To avoid these ambiguities, we will introduce the concept of a *synchronous data transformation*. The synchronous data transformation obeys the following set of conventions regarding its discrete data flows (prompts and connections to data stores are not considered in applying the conventions):

● At most one discrete input may exist.

● If the discrete input is a composite, all its elements must be present for the transformation to operate.

● Zero or more discrete outputs may exist.

● If there are two or more discrete outputs, they must be alternatives, and at most one may be produced for each operation of the transformation.

If the example of Figure 6.25 is rewritten using these conventions, each of the interpretations above requires a different schema. The schemas are shown in Figures 6.26, 6.27, and 6.28.

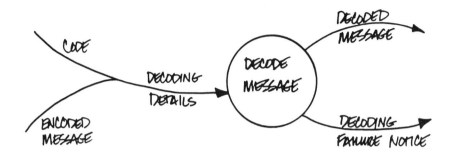

Figure 6.26. Unambiguous transformation, version 1.

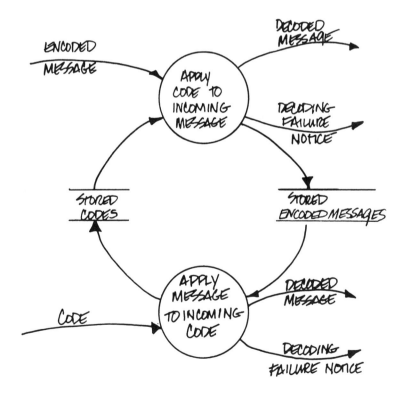

Figure 6.27. Unambiguous transformation, version 2.

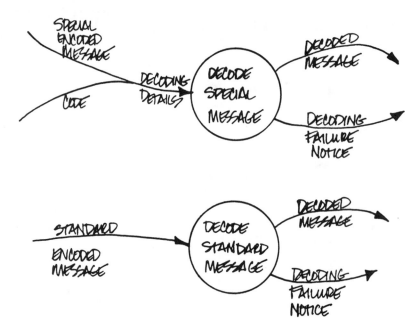

Figure 6.28. Unambiguous transformation, version 3.

6.10 Summary

The transformation schema is a network representation of the activity of a system. It allows a description that is rigorous and that encompasses both data relationships and the behavior of the system over time. However, there is a great deal of information relevant to the modeling of a system that cannot be conveniently be expressed by the transformation schema. Modeling tools to deal with other aspects of a system will be discussed in the following chapters.

Chapter 6: References

1. DeMarco, T. *Structured Analysis and System Specification.* (New York: Yourdon Press, 1978), pp. 47 ff.

Specifying Control Transformations

7.1 Basic concepts

The transformation schema describes the behavior of a system by giving names to transformations and showing the data and control connections among the transformations.

We have defined a notation for both data and control transformations and described the differences between them. We have also introduced the event flow and the control store as analogs of the data flow and the data store.

We must now concentrate on defining what a control transformation does, provide tools to model its behavior, and describe how it uses event flows and event stores.

7.2 The control transformation as a mapping

A control transformation maps input event flows into output event flows. Since event flows are fundamentally free of content — they simply occur at some discrete point in time, then go away — the transformation must combine the flow with internal memory to produce the selected output flow. The control transformation keeps track of what event flows have been received before and uses that information to produce its outputs. This can be illustrated with a trivial example such as a pull cord for a lamp. When the cord is pulled, the lamp may go on or off depending on what happened before, as shown in Figure 7.1.

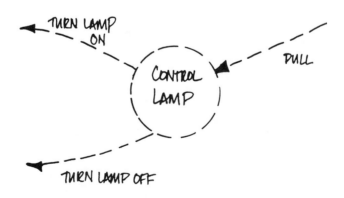

Figure 7.1. A simple control transformation.

We shall assume that each input event flow is completely processed before the next one can be processed. The processing involves a change in memory and the production of an output event flow. Clearly, it is possible to conceive of the past sequence of inputs as an infinite set of uniquely identifiable memory values. For example, we could think of the memory of the lamp-switch problem as being represented by an integer, which is incremented for each pull of the cord. All odd numbers have the lamp on, and all even numbers have the lamp off. This certainly is a correct representation, but there are only two different behaviors exhibited by the system: Think of the control transformation as recognizing only the two different behaviors of the lamp and as remembering which one of the two is being exhibited at any time. The sequence of events which produced the current behavior is not significant.

Thus, we characterize the *internal* memory of a control transformation in terms of the *externally* observable behavior of the system being controlled. At each point in time, the internal memory and the input event flow determine the output flows which, by their sequence, influence the externally observable behavior of the system. The internal memory changes as the output flows are produced so as to correspond to the changes in external behavior. Any single value for the internal memory must represent the same net external behavior.

7.3   Describing a control transformation

We shall describe, in this section, a specific model for defining the behavior of a control transformation — the state-transition diagram.

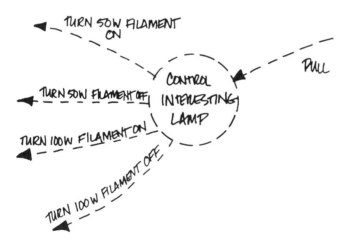

Figure 7.2. A more complex control transformation.

Consider a slightly more interesting lamp with two filaments, one of 100 W and another of 50 W. A single switch controls the lamp so that a sequence of cord pulls will turn the lamp from being off to providing illumination at 50 W then 100 W then 150 W then back to off (Figure 7.2). Externally, there are four behaviors. The event flow outputs have different implications for the system depending on when they occur. For example, turning the 50 W filament on may change the lamp from off to 50 W or it may change the lamp from 100 W to 150 W. A simple state-transition diagram for the two-filament lamp is shown in Figure 7.3. It is useful to think of the diagram as the "engine" that operates the control transformation.

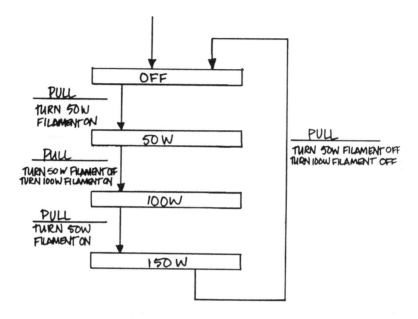

Figure 7.3. State transition diagram corresponding to Figure 7.2.

The components shown on this diagram are the state, represented by an elongated rectangle; the transition, represented by an arrow; the transition condition, shown adjacent to the transition above the line; and the transition action, shown adjacent to the transition below the line.

A *state* represents an externally observable mode of behavior. The name of the state is the name of the behavior exhibited by the system. Since we think of the state-transition diagram as modeling a control transformation, and no transformation work is occurring between transitions, we say that the state is passive. We can think of it as a manager or coordinator that is waiting for something to happen, so that it can then respond.

Each state represents a unique status of the control transformation's memory, and the transformations can be in only one state at a given time. One of the states on the state-transition diagram is designated as the *initial state* and is shown by a transition arrow pointing into the designated state with no source state ; conditions or actions may or may not be present. The initial state should be thought of as the behavior of the system before any transitions have occurred. One or more states on the state-transition diagram may be designated as *final states*. A final state has transition arrows entering but no transition arrows to other states, and should be thought of as a "dead end" in the behavior of the system.

Transitions represent the movement from one state to another. Transitions can exist between any state and any other state, including the state from which the transition started. A transition from a state to the *same* state would model the case that the net behavior of the system is the same both before and after the transition occurs.

Multiple transitions to and from a given state are permissible.

Both conditions and actions are associated with transitions.

Conditions cause the system to make a transition. We write the condition *above* a line that separates the condition and action of a transition. Each condition is identified with an input event flow that signals that the condition has occurred. The diagram does not describe the logic involved in computing the condition. A good way to read a condition is to say, "when <condition> occurs then...."

Actions are taken as the transition occurs. An action is a single indivisible activity which is identified with output event flow(s). Several independent actions may be taken on a single transition. They are all assumed to take place instantaneously and also to take place simultaneously unless an explicit sequence is indicated. For example, the two transitions in Figure 7.4 represent the same action. An interpretation equivalent to instantaneous carrying out of the actions is to say that nothing can happen on the transition from one state to another except the actions themselves.

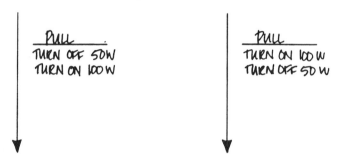

Figure 7.4. Equivalent transitions.

Actions may be null if the control transformation needs to remember the change in behavior but does not need to influence it.

7.4 Formal definition of the state-transition diagram

In formal terms, the notation just introduced defines a *finite automaton with output* [1]. This type of model consists of a set of states, one of which is the initial state and some of which may be final states, an alphabet of input symbols, an alphabet of output symbols, and a transition function that maps combinations of states and input symbols into states. (In our use of this model, both the input and output alphabets are associated with sets of event flows.)

A finite automaton with output may be organized in one of two ways. A *Moore machine* is an automaton in which each *state* is associated with an output symbol; a *Mealy machine* associates each *transition* (that is, each combination of state and input symbol) with an output symbol.

We have used states to represent intervals of time over which some behavior persists and transitions to represent points in time at which behavior changes. We have therefore chosen to use the Mealy model, since our output symbols, the event flows, are also localized at points in time.

The most common graphic representation of a finite automaton uses circles for states and arrows for transitions. Because of the potential for confusion between transformation schemas and state-transition diagrams, we have chosen not to use this representation.

We shall now examine an alternative way of transmitting essentially the same information about a control transformation.

7.5 State transition and action tables

The information in Figure 7.5 may also be represented by constructing a *state-transition table* where columns are conditions, rows represent the current state, and the intersection of a row and a column defines the new state produced when the condition occurs in the current state. The table corresponding to Figure 7.5 is shown in Figure 7.6. The blank entries are interpreted to mean that we shall stay in the same state when the condition occurs. The principal advantage of this scheme is that it forces us to consider all possible conditions for each state. For example, what should occur if a "stop" event occurs when "flushing"?

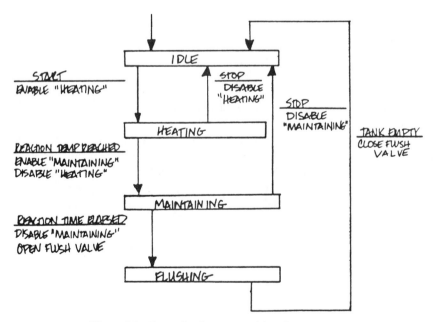

Figure 7.5. Example of state transition diagram.

	START	STOP	TANK EMPTY	REACTION TEMP REACHED	REACTION TIME ELAPSED
IDLE	HEATING				
HEATING		IDLE		MAINTAINING	
MAINTAINING		IDLE			FLUSHING
FLUSHING			IDLE		

Figure 7.6. Transition table for Figure 7.5.

Action tables serve as a companion technique to denote the actions, as shown in Figure 7.7. The two tables may be combined into a single one, which puts all the information in one place but which may make reading difficult.

The principal disadvantage of the technique is that if the number of transitions is small in comparision to the number of states multiplied by the number of conditions, then the table is quite large, but relatively sparse. To be fair, the state-transition diagram suffers from the inverse problem: if many transitions are permitted between a small number of states, the diagram can become hopelessly tangled.

	START	STOP	TANK EMPTY	REACTION TEMP REACHED	REACTION TIME ELAPSED
IDLE	ENABLE "HEATING"				
HEATING		DISABLE "HEATING"		DISABLE "HEATING" ENABLE "MAINTAINING"	
MAINTAINING		DISABLE "MAINTAINING"			DISABLE "MAINTAINING" OPEN FLUSH VALVE
FLUSHING			CLOSE FLUSH VALVE		

Figure 7.7. Action table for Figure 7.5.

7.6 Connections to data transformations

A control transformation can issue event flows whose effect is to enable, disable, or trigger a data transformation. Control transformations can therefore be formulated in terms of the starting and stopping of other transformations. This has two major implications, as follows: The destination of some event flows must be encoded in the definition of a control transformation. The logic of the data transformations can be defined independently of the circumstances that cause them to run.

The allocation of the coordination role to a control transformation relieves the data transformation of the coordination responsibility. A control transformation, by its nature, must be aware of other activities in the schema. After all, it is the job of the control transformation to manage them. This information is encoded on the logic that represents the control transformation. Separating data and control transformations allows easier comprehension of both functions.

7.7 Reducing complexity

Certain situations that commonly occur in systems can greatly increase the complexity of a state-transition diagram. Consider modifying the system shown in Figure 7.5 so that the flushing must be preceded by an "authorizing" event flow. Suppose also that the flow can occur any time after the start signal, either before or after the reaction time has elapsed. The state-transition diagram must be modified so that the Flush Tank event flow can be remembered for later use if it occurs during the Heating or Maintaining states. One such modification is shown in Figure 7.8. Notice the great increase in the complexity of the model. We will use the event store mechanism to avoid complex state models in situations such as this.

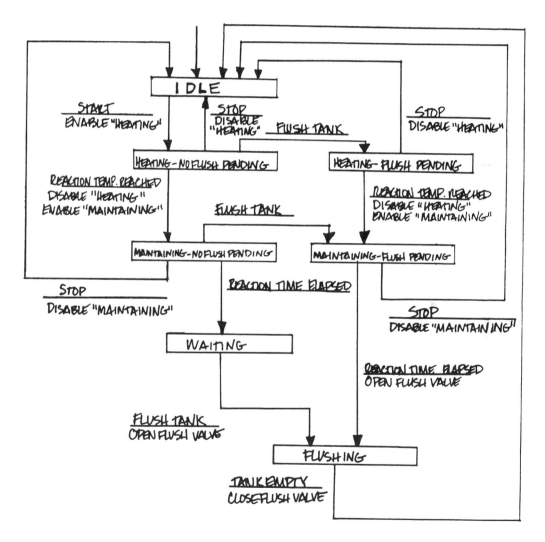

Figure 7.8. Effect of time-delayed response to an event flow.

The event store is used to remember information about events that have occurred but are not yet to be used. There are three operations defined that affect the event store, as illustrated in Figure 7.9. The Reset operation changes the value of the store to its initial value and also cancels any Process Wait in progress. The Signal operation increases the value of the store by one. The Process Wait operation carries out the following logic:

>decrement value of store by 1
>if value of store $\geq$ 0 then
>>issue "Pass"
>
>else
>>do until (signal)
>>>wait
>>
>>issue "Pass"

The event store is equivalent to a *semaphore* as defined by Dijkstra [2].

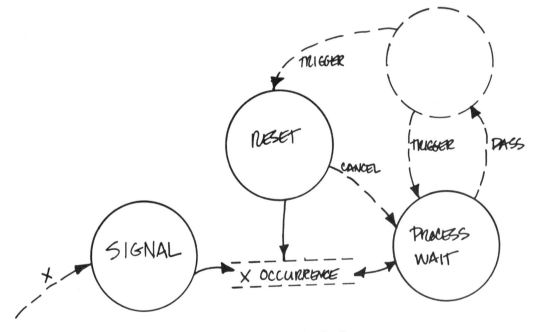

Figure 7.9. Control store operation details.

All three operations are completely independent of the meaning of what is stored. To avoid needless repetitions of this logic, the event store is represented in the short-hand form shown in Figure 7.10. Using an event store, we can model the control transformation as shown in Figure 7.11. The event store remembers that the Flush Tank event flow has occurred, even though it may not be used until much later in the process. Figure 7.12 shows the modified state-transition diagram, assuming that the tank is not flushed if the reaction is stopped abnormally.

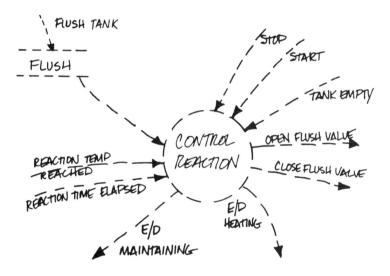

Figure 7.10. Control store shorthand notation.

Figure 7.11. Control transformation with event store.

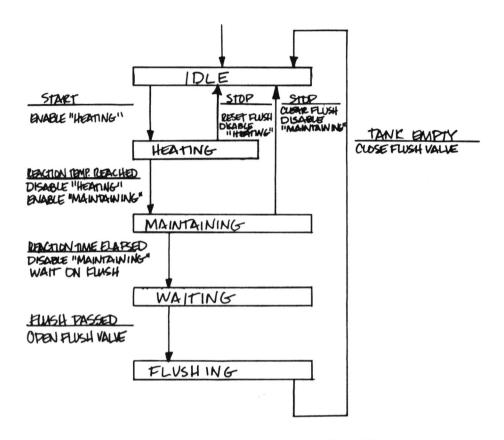

Figure 7.12. State transition diagram for Figure 7.11.

Another situation that can complicate a state-transition diagram is a large number of similar behaviors of the system being controlled. Consider a system that must keep track of train traffic in a tunnel. If the tunnel is long enough to accommodate four trains simultaneously, the situation could be represented as in Figure 7.13. The model is awkward and highly redundant; furthermore, if the system were to be implemented in several tunnels with differing capacities, a general model could not be built.

A shorthand notation for this situation is shown in Figure 7.14. The tests, increments, and decrements of the counter T are not true conditions and actions, but merely a concise way of representing a number of similar states.

Even with these conventions for simplification, a single state diagram for a complex system can be very large. An alternative representation is discussed in the next section.

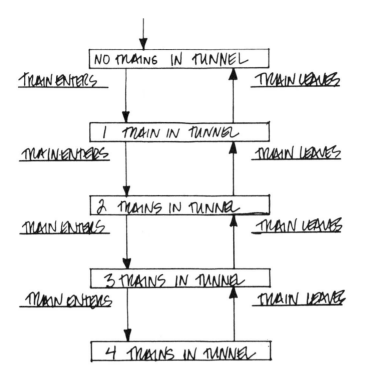

Figure 7.13. Multiple similar states.

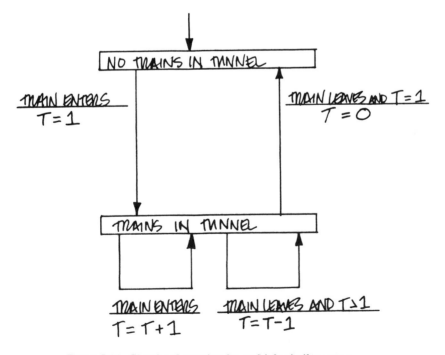

Figure 7.14. Shorthand notation for multiple similar states.

7.8 Connections between control transformations

Control transformations interact with other components of the transformation schema. We have described the interactions between control transformations and event flows as well as the management role played with respect to data transformations. We now turn to the interactions between control transformations.

Let us begin with the simplest interaction of all — none. If two control transformations do not communicate, then both can be thought of as operating separately and asynchronously. The system as a whole is in a state that is a compound of the states of the individual control transformations. The total number of possible states is the product of the number of states in each control transformation.

Control transformations may receive event flows from other control transformations, just as they may receive them from outside the system. As with data transformations, the source of the flow is not relevant to the transformation. We could change the boundary of the system to exclude the control transformation that issues the event flow, and the receiving control transformation cannot tell the difference. In any case, an event flow would affect the behavior of the receiving control transformation, and so the behavior of the sender and receiver would be linked, as in the example of Figure 7.15. The associated state-transition diagrams are shown in Figure 7.16; the state-transition diagram on the right cannot change states until it receives the event flow from the left-hand state transition diagram.

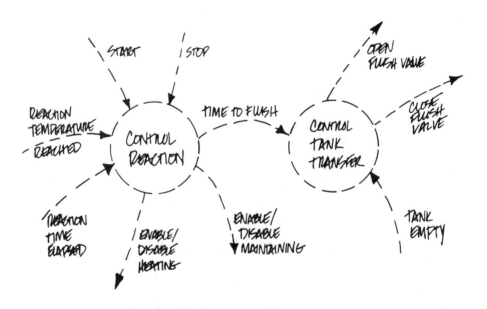

Figure 7.15. Coordination between control transformations.

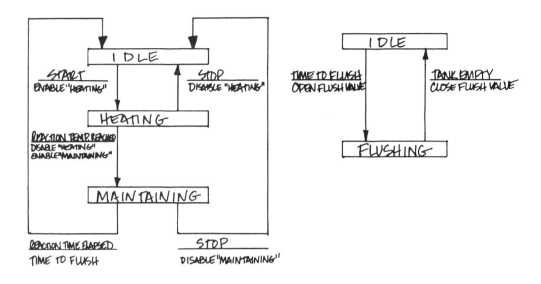

Figure 7.16. State transition diagrams for Figure 7.15.

Although we can still conceptualize the overall state of the system as the combination of the states of the two control transformations, some combinations of states are now prohibited because of the interaction between the two sets of states.

The two control transformations of Figure 7.16 are equivalent to the single one of Figure 7.5; the Time to Flush event flow is an artifact of the partitioning, it serves as an action for the sending diagram and as a condition for the receiving diagram.

We choose between the two alternative representations on the basis of complexity. We split the model into two if a single model is too complex to understand, and we merge two models into one if the complexity introduced by the partitioning (as shown by the flows between the two models) outweighs the complexity of a single model.

In addition to receiving input event flows, control transformations can also be enabled/disabled by other control transformations. This is shown by an outgoing prompt-type control flow in the same way as for data transformations. When a control transformation is enabled, we can regard the enabled control transformation as being brought into existence and started up in the same way as a data transformation. The control transformation starts in its initial state. As described in Chapter 6, we can extend this idea to include multiple instances of the same state model. For example, a bottling system may have several bottling lines. Each line is the same, so we draw just one state model for a bottling line. However, each line can be in its own state separately and independently from the other bottling lines, and thus each control transformation will be in its own state. The overall state of the system is the combination of the states of *all instances* of the control transformations.

When a control transformation is disabled, the conventions are as follows: Any transformations or activities outside the schema that have been enabled by the control transformation are disabled. The state of the control transformation becomes undefined.

7.9 Modeling complex dynamics

The modeling ideas introduced in the preceding two sections — event stores, counters to track similar states, and using multiple control transformations — can be used together to model relatively complex situations concisely and rigorously. Let's use as an example two pairs of tracks that coalesce into one to traverse a tunnel (Figure 7.17). As trains approach the tunnel, they hit a sensor that announces their presence, then stop at the stop light until/unless it is green. Once traffic has begun in one direction, the light for that direction remains green, and additional trains may enter freely. The light turns red again when the last train has left. Meanwhile, a train approaching from the other direction must wait until the opposing traffic has ended. Figures 7.18 and 7.19 represent the control transformations and the associated state diagrams for the control system. The event store has an initial value of 1.

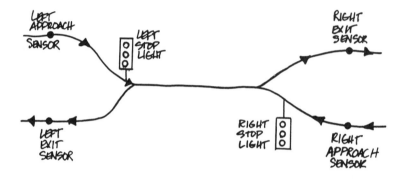

Figure 7.17. Train traffic control problems.

7.10 Summary

The state-transition diagram describes the logic of a control transformation. Whether represented graphically or in tabular form, it permits a precise interpretation of the system's response to events over the course of time.

In the next chapter, we will take up the description of data transformation logic.

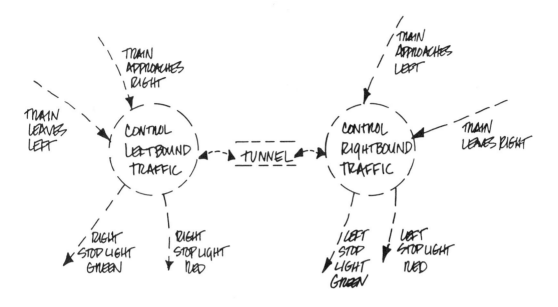

Figure 7.18. Control transformations for Figure 7.17.

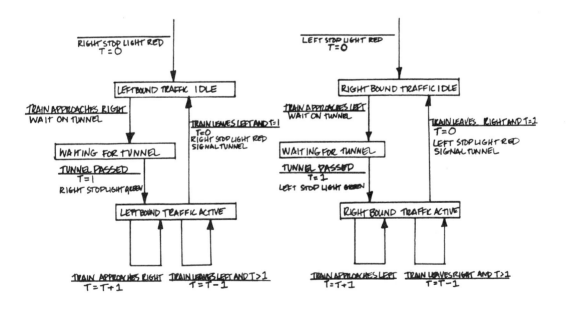

Figure 7.19. State transition diagrams for Figure 7.18.

Chapter 7: References

1. Hopcroft, J.E. and Ullman, J.D., *Introduction to Automata Theory, Languages, and Computation.* (Reading: Addison-Wesley Publishing Company, 1979), pp. 16-45.

2. Dijkstra, E.W., " Cooperating Sequential Processes," *Programming Languages,* ed. F. Genuys (New York: Academic Press, 1968).

8
Specifying Data Transformations

8.1 Introduction

The graphic representation used in a transformation schema is not sufficient to produce a rigorous description of a data transformation. The schema represents the inputs to and outputs from the data transformation, but the only description of the transformation's behavior is its name. In a simple transformation such as shown in Figure 8.1, the omission of details about the transformation isn't much of a problem; its behavioral requirements are intuitively obvious. Figure 8.2 presents a completely different situation. The transformation must schedule a series of machine operations to produce a quantity of some finished product. The schedule must not conflict with existing schedules and must minimize the overall non-productive time for the entire set of machines. It is not nearly so obvious what or how much additional detail must be added so that the model can be used as the basis for a successful implementation.

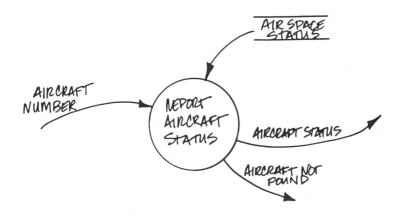

Figure 8.1. A simple data transformation.

The precondition for creating a specification for a data transformation is that the data used and produced by the transformation be completely specified. The identity of the data items contained in the data stores and in any composite flow must be stated, along with any structural relationship among data items (for example, multiple instances or mutual exclusion of items within a flow). Chapter 11, Specifying Data, provides details on what is required.

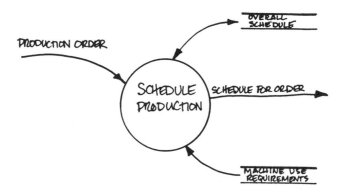

Figure 8.2. A complex data transformation.

Once the details of the input and output data are known, one of two fundamentally different approaches can be taken. Most transformation descriptions illustrated by DeMarco [1] and others are sets of rules for calculating the values of the outputs of a transformation if the values of the inputs are provided. Although De Marco cautions against specifying transformations in a way that is unduly constraining to the designer or implementer, many of his examples of "minispecifications" are in fact informal procedural algorithms. The danger of this approach, if it is used for requirements definition, is simply that one can fall into the trap of producing a specification that is implementation oriented rather than problem oriented. The set of rules required to construct the output values is often written as a group of statements in which the order of execution is crucial to the correct operation of the transformation; that is, the specification is fundamentally *procedural*. Since many of today's automated processors are procedural, and the degree of precision required to produce a specification is much like that of writing code, it is all too easy to specify *how* the transformation may be implemented, rather than *what* it needs to do.

The second approach is to write the specification in a *non-procedural* manner. This type of specification focuses on criteria for measuring whether or not an implementation would be a correct solution to the problem. Contrast two specifications for a transformation that computes the square root of its input; the first provides a set of rules for going about the computation and the second simply states that the input must be the square of the output to an accuracy of ten decimal places. Most specifications fall somewhere between the two extremes: there is a continuum of possible specification techniques. In subsequent sections of this chapter, we shall describe some of these techniques, and we shall point to the advantages and disadvantages of each.

8.2 Building procedural specifications using a high-level language

As mentioned in the previous section, one of the most straightforward ways to describe a transformation is to give a set of rules for carrying it out. For example, a program could be written in a high-level language such as Ada or Pascal which, when executed, will produce quantitatively correct outputs for inputs to the transformation.

Input and output flows and stores can be replaced by simple file structures. No attempt need be made in this situation to simulate the actual implementation environment. Both the ultimate programming language and the ultimate target machine may be different from the specification as written. Furthermore, constraints such as required timings and precision of numeric variables need not be adhered to.

8.3 Other procedural techniques

A Program Design Language (PDL) is a (usually textual) representation of transformation logic that has a rigorously defined syntax but that is not meant to be executed by a computer. PDL's may be specifically designed for their function, or a high-level language such as Ada or Pascal may be used as a PDL. In the latter case, the syntax of the high-level language is used, but those features of the language and the supporting system software required for execution are omitted.

When a PDL is used, the compilation features of a high-level language are available and may be used to identify structural logic errors (like undefined loop boundaries), data naming inconsistencies, and similar problems. Furthermore, system library services for storage and modification of source code may also be used for PDL statements. A PDL description may also be executed. However, the execution must be done by a group of people in a paper-and-pencil fashion. As with executable code, various input values may be tried, the resulting output values manually calculated, and the results used for refinement. The prior creation of a transformation schema enhances the usefulness of a PDL, as it does for executable code, by making the PDL sections smaller and better defined.

Pseudocode refers to a textual representation that has a somewhat formal syntax but for which no machine compilation facilities are available (usually because the syntax is chosen in an ad-hoc manner by an organization or a project team). Pseudocode has the same features as a PDL, except that both compilation (structural logic checking) and execution must be done manually.

Let's specify the transformation shown in Figure 8.3 using pseudocode. The Planes store contains the Plane ID Number, Owner's Name, and Plane Type for a set of planes. The Airports store contains the Airport ID, Airport Name, and Airport Classification for a set of airports. The Landings store contains the Time and Weather Conditions for a set of landings; each landing is associated with a plane and an airport from the other sets. The Landing Report Request contains a Weather Condition value, a Plane Type value, and an Airport Classification value. Finally, the Landing Report consists of a set of entries containing Plane ID Number, Owner's Name, Airport ID, Airport Name, and Time for the specified Weather Condition, Plane Type, and Airport Classification.

A pseudocode specification for the transformation is:
        Do Until (ENDFILE)
            Readsequential (PLANE) from (PLANES)
            if PLANE.PLANETYPE = INPUT.PLANETYPE
            then
                Do Until (ENDASSOCIATIONS)
                    Findassociated (LANDING) for (PLANE)
                    if LANDING.WEATHERCONDITION =
                    INPUT.WEATHERCONDITION
                    then
                        Findassociated (AIRPORT) for (LANDING)
                        If AIRPORT.AIRPORTCLASSIFICATION =
                        INPUT.AIRPORTCLASSIFICATION
                        then
                            put PLANEIDNUMBER, OWNERSNAME, AIRPORTID,
                        AIRPORTNAME, TIME into LANDINGREPORT
        Write (LANDINGREPORT)

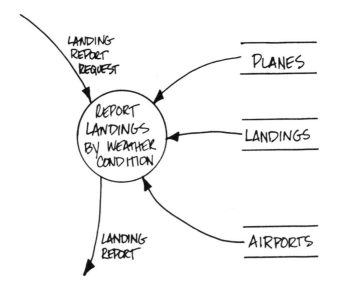

Figure 8.3. Transformation to be specified.

ENDFILE and ENDASSOCIATIONS are internal variables used to describe the outcome of data access attempts, with possible values of "true" and "false." Capitalization is used to differentiate data variables from words describing operations and tests on data.

Structured English as defined by DeMarco [2] is fundamentally a relaxed form of pseudocode. It uses a subset of English (or any other nautral language) that is formal and restricted enough to be unambiguous to a reader but that has no precise syntactic requirements. Structured English has the following characteristics: It refers only to variable data elements or groups that are defined as contained in the flows and stores connected to the transformation or are strictly internal (intermediate products). It uses clear imperatives such as "find", "store", "select the largest", and so on, to refer to operations on data elements and groups. It connects operations on data elements only with *structured programming* constructs (sequence, if-then-else, various closed loop constructions). It uses indentation, numbering, or some equivalent notation to clarify the structure of the logic.

Here is a Structured English description equivalent to the preceding pseudocode:

For each PLANE with PLANE TYPE matching the input PLANE TYPE
   (1) Find each associated LANDING with WEATHER CONDITION
      matching the input WEATHER CONDITION
   (2) For each LANDING found
      (2.1) Find the associated AIRPORT
      (2.2) If the AIRPORT CLASSIFICATION matches the input
         AIRPORT CLASSIFICATION
        then
            add PLANE ID NUMBER, OWNERS NAME, AIRPORT ID,
            AIRPORT NAME, and TIME to LANDING REPORT
   Issue LANDING REPORT

All the procedural specifications illustrated in the previous sections consist of *rules* or *instructions* for creating outputs from inputs. Specifying by instructions requires the selection of a single set of rules. If there is more than one set of instructions capable of producing correct outputs, an implementation bias will be created.

Both the pseudocode and the Structured English descriptions just presented contain such an implementation bias. The extraction of the output data involves an access path that goes from the Plane store through the Landing store to the Airport store. An equally correct procedure involves a path in the opposite direction, from Airport through Landing to Plane. The Structured English specification in this case would be the following:

> For each AIRPORT with AIRPORT CLASSIFICATION
> matching the input AIRPORT CLASSIFICATION
> > (1) Find each associated LANDING with WEATHER CONDITION
> > matching the input WEATHER CONDITION
> > (2) For each LANDING found
> > > (2.1) Find the associated PLANE
> > > (2.2) If the PLANE TYPE matches the input PLANE TYPE
> > > then
> > > > add PLANE ID NUMBER, OWNERS NAME, AIRPORT ID,
> > > > AIRPORT NAME, and TIME to LANDING REPORT
> Issue LANDING REPORT

There is yet another correct procedure, which involves a path from Landing to both Plane and Airport.

The relative efficiency of these three procedures depends on the relative number of occurrences of each type of stored data and also on the nature of the stored data connections as actually implemented. If these factors aren't known at requirements definition time, and if the implementer doesn't recognize the arbitrary nature of the procedure, a sub-optimal implementation could result.

We shall now turn our attention to less procedural forms of specification.

8.4 Graphic and tabular specifications

The creation of a combinatorial specification is possible when the output of a transformation consists of a data element with discrete values and when the output values are determined directly by values or ranges of values of the input data elements.

Figure 8.4 shows a transformation that categorizes synthetic fiber test results in terms of denier (fiber thickness) and tensile strength. Figure 8.5 describes this transformation in terms of a *decision tree*. (An equivalent tabular representation may also be used and is illustrated in DeMarco [3].) Although this tree is easy to translate into a set of instructions for producing outputs, it does not *prescribe* a set of instructions; it may be implemented either by a look-up table or by if-then-else logic.

Figure 8.4. A combinatorial transformation.

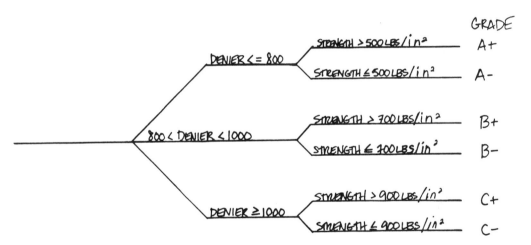

Figure 8.5. A decision tree specification.

A state-transition diagram or table is another graphic specification tool that may be used when output flows have discrete values. Although the state transition diagram is particularly useful for describing control transformations, it may also be used to describe data transformations. Figure 8.6 reads an input character stream and outputs either legal integers, legal decimal numbers, or illegal combinations; blanks serve as separators. Figure 8.7 represents the logic of the transformation. Like the decision tree, it is easily realized as specific instructions but does not prescribe any specific set of instructions.

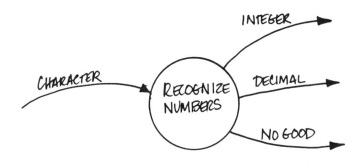

Figure 8.6. Numeric editing transformation.

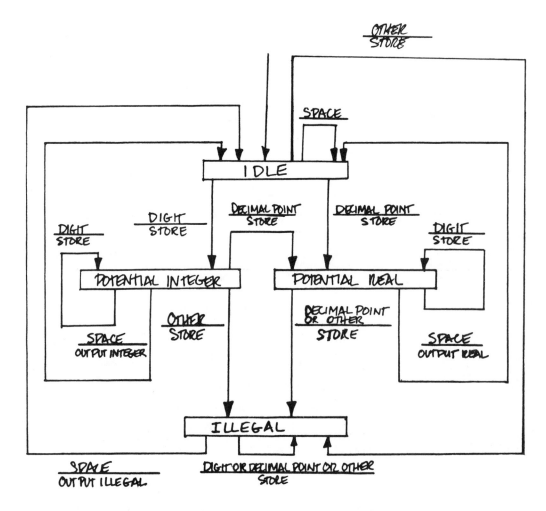

Figure 8.7. State transition diagram for Figure 8.6.

8.5 Precondition-postcondition specifications

A particularly powerful specification method involves relating conditions on input values to corresponding conditions on output values. In general, more than one precondition-postcondition combination is needed. Let's return to the example of Figure 8.1 and express its specification in this form:

(1) AIRCRAFT NUMBER &
AIRCRAFT NUMBER in AIRCRAFT STATUS(i) of AIRSPACE STATUS
--->
AIRCRAFT STATUS(i) & not AIRCRAFT NOT FOUND

(2) AIRCRAFT NUMBER &
AIRCRAFT NUMBER not in any AIRCRAFT STATUS of AIRSPACE STATUS
--->
not AIRCRAFT STATUS & AIRCRAFT NOT FOUND

The first statement can be read as, If there is an AIRCRAFT NUMBER input and the AIRCRAFT NUMBER value matches any instance of AIRCRAFT STATUS, the output should be that instance rather than AIRCRAFT NOT FOUND. The second statement has a similar interpretation. This representation is like state-transition diagrams and decision trees in that it specifies relationships between input and outputs without listing rules for producing the outputs.

It is interesting to ask whether this is a *complete* specification; that is, whether it covers all possible input conditions. As a matter of fact, the two preconditions cover all possible combinations of inputs and stored data values. However, this does not mean that the specification is satisfactory. It is also necessary that the preconditions don't overlap — otherwise two or more contradictory output conditions might be specified for an input condition. Furthermore, the input conditions must not be too general. Referring to the preconditions just given, for example, what happens if there is *more than one instance* in AIRSPACE STATUS of an AIRCRAFT STATUS with a matching number? The first precondition-postcondition indicates that a single AIRCRAFT STATUS will be output, but which one?

There are several options for dealing with this situation. The AIRCRAFT STATUS output flow can be modified to allow multiple instances, an extra MULTIPLE INSTANCE ERROR output flow can be added to the transformation, or the specifier can pass the buck by appealing to the specification of the AIRSPACE STATUS store and denying responsibility for multiple instances. In any case the specification can be modified easily. To handle the last of the options, the first statement must be qualified to specify only a single match, and an additional statement must be added, as follows:
AIRCRAFT NUMBER &
AIRCRAFT NUMBER in AIRCRAFT STATUS(i) of AIRSPACE STATUS &
AIRCRAFT NUMBER in AIRCRAFT STATUS(j) of AIRSPACE STATUS & j ≠ i
--->
(output not defined)

This is a perfectly valid specification, although perhaps not a very satisfactory resolution.

Some progress has been made in creating precondition-postcondition descriptions for non-trivial transformations that are provably complete and correct (see for example Parnas, et al [4]). However, this is in general a very difficult task.

Transformations that represent the controlling portion of a control loop, such as in Figure 8.8, are an interesting variation on the precondition-postcondition idea. Here the values of the Throttle Control output aren't of any special interest. What's of interest is the *behavior of the speed over time*. A specification for this type of transformation can be expressed as preconditions at some point in time and postconditions at later times. For example:

| SPEED - SPEED SETPOINT | < 2 mph at T = 0 &
ENGINE RESPONSE DELAY < 0.25 sec for T > 0
--->
| SPEED - SPEED SETPOINT | < 2 mph for T > 0

This can be read as, If at some point in time the speed matches the speed setpoint (desired speed) within 2 mph and if from that point on the engine responds to a change in throttle position after less than 0.25 seconds, the speed will remain within 2 mph of the speed setpoint. This is a peculiar specification in that the transformation can be made to "misbehave" by changes in the systems environment (for example the engine-response delay).

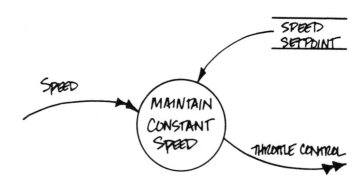

Figure 8.8. A transformation performing closed-loop control.

As a final point on precondition-postcondition specifications, note that the notation is quite general and can be used to represent both decision trees and state-transition diagrams. In the state diagram case, the precondition specifies the condition and the initial state, and the postcondition specifies the action and the final state.

8.6 Reverse transformation specifications

There is a large class of transformations that are required to *undo* a sequence of transformations that were applied to data previous to input. Heitmeyer and McLean [5] have developed a method for specifying the required processing in terms of *reversing* the set of external transformations applied prior to input. Suppose that the input to a transformation consists of a set of messages that were first encrypted and then multiplexed. The specification would rigorously describe the details of the encryption and the multiplexing. The implementer would satisfy the specification by creating an *inverse* for the sequence of pre-input transformations. Notice that the method does *not* prescribe inverting the transformations in reverse order — that is, demultiplexing followed by decoding. Any algorithm that, given an encrypted and multiplexed input, can reproduce the original messages will satisfy the specification.

8.7 Summary

The specification for a data transformation describes the required relationships between inputs and outputs. The specification may be stated procedurally — in terms of a set of rules for deriving outputs from inputs. It is also possible to create a non-procedural specification that describes the required input/output relationships without giving derivation rules.

Chapter 8: References

1. T. DeMarco. *Structured Analysis and System Specification.* New York: Yourdon Press, 1978, pp. 169-226.

2. Ibid., pp. 179-213.

3. Ibid, pp. 215-226.

4. D.L. Parnas, W. Bartussek, G. Handzel, and H. Wuerges, "Using Predicate Transformers to Verify the Effects of Real Programs," TR 76-101, University of North Carolina at Chapel Hill and Technische Hochschule Darmstadt, Oct. 27, 1976.

5. C.L. Heitmeyer and J.D. McLean. "Abstract Requirements Specification: A New Approach and Its Application," *IEEE Transactions on Software Engineering,* Vol. SE-9, No. 5 (Sept. 1983), pp. 580-589.

Executing the Transformation Schema

9.1 Introduction

Despite our support for the use of graphics in system modeling, we are aware that problems have arisen in systems development because of misuse of graphic-modeling notations. The mere use of a standard set of symbols does not assure that a graphic model will be internally consistent or unambiguous.

The problem of misuse of descriptive tools is obviously not confined to graphics. The use of written text is notorious for uncontrolled redundancy, internal inconsistency, and the possibility of multiple interpretations. However, great strides have been made in ensuring the rigorous use of text. A high-level programming language is simply a formalized natural-language subset whose interpretation and validation rules are enforceable by an automated processor.

There is no reason why a graphic description language need be less rigorous than a textual one. We have defined the transformation schema as a formalized graphics language with a set of interpretation and validation rules similar to those for a programming language. We can think of application of these rules as "compiling," both for the programming language and for the schema.

It is true that until fairly recently the limitations of computer technology made "graphics compilers" and "graphics executors" impractical. Recently, workstations for computer-aided design have made it possible for a mechanical engineer to enter a graphic description of a metal part and then have it checked for geometric consistency and have the part produced by a computer-driven machine tool without human intervention. However, the basic issue is not automatability but formalization.

In Chapter 6, Modeling Transformations, we introduced "compilation" rules by which a transformation schema can be shown to be internally consistent. However, the bottom-line test of a set of a programming language statements is not its compilability but its *executability* -- the demonstration that a machine can correctly interpret the statements as a procedure for creating outputs from inputs. It is our purpose in this chapter to show how a schema that meets the compilation rules can be *executed;* that is, made to simulate or predict at some level of detail the behavior of the system being modeled. The most convenient implementation of these ideas is an automated systems development workstation. However, a schema can be executed by people working with paper-and-pencil, and the process has significant payoffs in understanding the system being modeled. The execution of the schema is based on the description of the execution of the Petri net given by Peterson [1].

There are three levels at which a transformation schema may be executed: the schematic level, the prototype level, and the direct-implementation level. The remaining sections of the chapter will describe the basics of execution and then the specifics of each execution level.

9.2 Definition of execution of a data transformation

The execution of a synchronous data transformation is illustrated in Figure 9.1. (We will assume that data corresponding to the aircraft number is present in the store; the consequences of the breakdown of this assumption will be treated in section 9.5. See the discussion of Figure 9.10.) The condition for the execution of this transformation is simply the arrival of an instance of its input flow, which is represented by the placement of a *token* — the filled-in square — on the input flow. The token may be regarded as being associated with a specific value of the data element(s) in the input flow, but it need not be. As soon as its condition is fulfilled, the transformation executes, which should be conceived of as happening in zero time. The result of the execution is the removal of the token from the input flow and its placement on the output flow. Like the input token, the output token may or may not be associated with a value for the output flow.

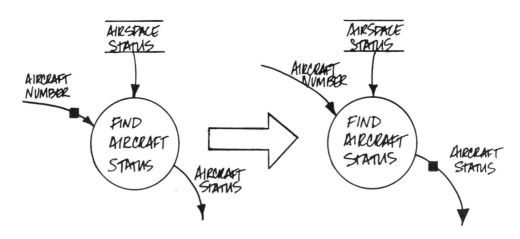

Figure 9.1. Execution of a simple transformation.

The execution of a transformation schema becomes somewhat more complex when transformations can be enabled and disabled by prompts. The representation of the enable/disable mechanism is illustrated in Figure 9.2. In part (a) of the figure, a token is placed on the Enable prompt of a previously disabled transformation. The processing of the prompt causes the token on the Enable flow to be removed, and a token to be placed on the transformation itself to indicate that it is currently enabled. Part (b) of the figure shows the reverse procedure. Placing a token on the Disable flow of a currently enabled transformation results in the removal of both tokens, and the resulting absence of a token on the transformation shows it is currently disabled. (Enabling a currently enabled transformation, or disabling a currently disabled transformation, is treated as an error).

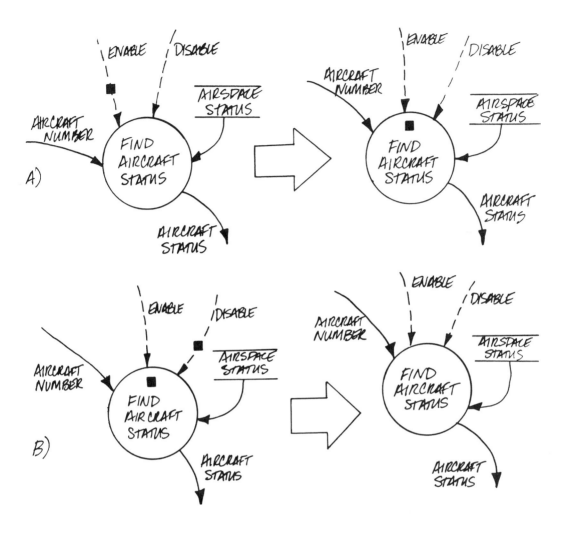

Figure 9.2. Enabling/disabling of a transformation.

The prior enabling or disabling of a transformation influences its response to a token placed on an input flow. In part (a) of Figure 9.3, the arrival of a discrete data input causes a previously enabled transformation to produce an output. In part (b) of the figure, the input token is simply discarded, and no output is produced, because the transformation is not enabled.

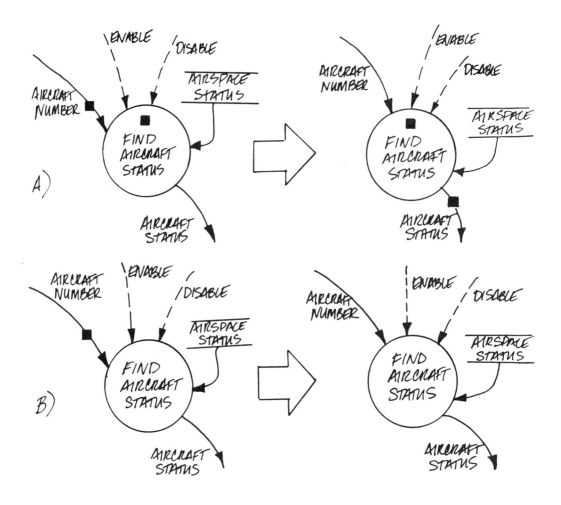

Figure 9.3. Effect of enabling/disabling on action of a transformation.

Figure 9.4 represents a situation where the transformation has time-continuous input and output flows. For time-continuous output flows, the absence of a token means that the transformation is not producing the flow, and the presence of a token means that the flow has some value. A time-continuous input flow from outside the schema is assumed always to have a token and always has a value. When a transformation has a continuous output data flow and Enable/Disable flows, its output is prohibited as long as the transformation is disabled. When the transformation is enabled, as shown in Figure 9.4, it may begin producing output values.

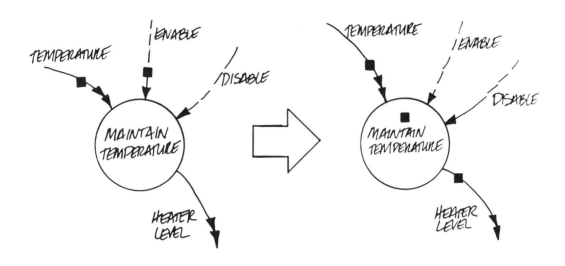

Figure 9.4. Transformation with continuous flows.

Table 9.1 shows the interpretation of tokens for various types of flows.

PLACEMENT OF TOKEN	INTERPRETATION WHEN PRESENT	INTERPRETATION WHEN ABSENT
TIME-DISCRETE INPUT DATA FLOW	AN INPUT HAS ARRIVED	NO INPUT HAS ARRIVED
TIME-DISCRETE OUTPUT DATA FLOW	AN OUTPUT HAS BEEN PRODUCED*	NO OUTPUT HAS BEEN PRODUCED
TIME-CONTINUOUS INPUT DATA FLOW	INPUT HAS A VALUE (ALWAYS PRESENT)	N/A
TIME-CONTINUOUS OUTPUT DATA FLOW	OUTPUT IS BEING PRODUCED	OUTPUT IS NOT BEING PRODUCED
EVENT FLOW	A PROMPT HAS ARRIVED	NO PROMPT HAS ARRIVED
TRANSFORMATION	INPUTS WILL BE ACCEPTED	NO INPUTS WILL BE ACCEPTED

* token must be cleared before next execution of transformation that
produced the output.

Table 9.1   Interpretation of tokens.

Let's look at the execution of a data transformation that produces only discrete
outputs. As shown in Figure 9.5, there are two varieties of transformations; those that
can guarantee the availability of their data at all times — such as, 9.5 (a) and (b), and
those that cannot, (c) and (d). In the case of (a) and (b), the transformations are capable of producing output at any time. However, we require the output at a specific
point in time, so we show the event flow as a *trigger*. The output is produced the in-

stant the transformation is prompted and does not reappear till the next trigger. On the other hand, the capability of transformations like (c) and (d) to produce discrete outputs depends both on previously received event flows and on either the instantaneous occurrence of, or the attainment of a specific value by, an input data flow. For this reason we label the event flows as *enable* and *disable*. Note that in the case of transformation 9.5 (c), data is *drawn from* the store only when the discrete input flow arrives. Let's now look at the execution of a control transformation.

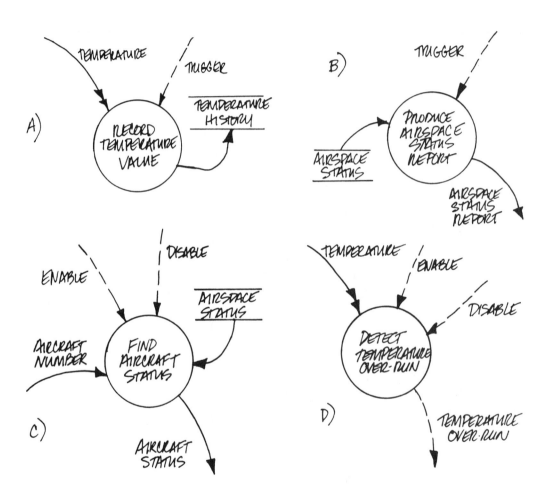

Figure 9.5. Discrete-output transformations.

9.3 Definition of execution of a control transformation

The execution of a data transformation as defined above does not require the existence of a transformation specification. However, the execution of a control transformation is not defined unless there is a state-transition diagram (or some equivalent representation) associated with the transformation. Execution of the transformation is actually execution of the state diagram.

A control transformation is prepared for execution when a token has been placed to indicate the state of its associated state diagram. The absence of a token is legitimate when the control transformation is enabled and disabled by another control transformation; the absence indicates that the transformation is currently inactive and will not respond to event flows. The condition for execution of an enabled control transformation is a token placed on an input event flow. The result of execution is a possible change in position of the token marking the state and possible placement of tokens on output event flows.

In Figure 9.6, the arrival of an instance of A causes the state to change from X to Y and places tokens on two Enable/Disable output flows.

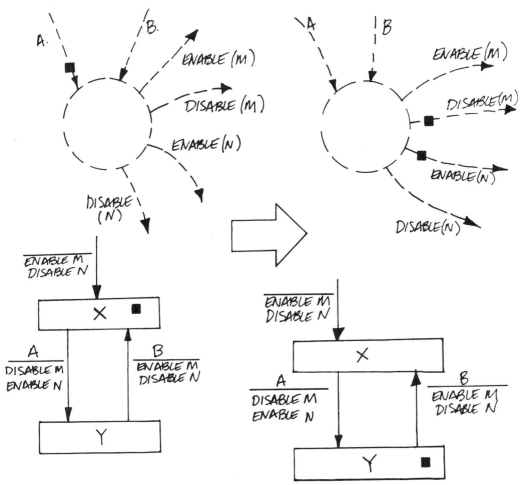

Figure 9.6. Execution of a control transformation.

If a control transformation is in a state in which no response to a particular event flow is defined, the arrival of that event flow results in the discarding of the token, with no action taken.

As we described in Chapter 7, control stores are *active* components of the schema. When a token is placed on an event flow that is an input to a control store, the token is placed into the store. (There may be more than one token in the store.) If a "wait on" is pending, a token from the store is immediately placed on the event flow that triggers the pass condition for the control transformation with the oldest outstanding "wait on," and that control transformation is executed. Similarly, if a control transformation waits on a control store, and there are one or more tokens in the store, a token is placed on the event flow that triggers the pass condition. Otherwise, no action is taken.

9.4 Effects of simultaneous token placement/removal

Since a transformation schema may have multiple input flows, it is possible to envision placing tokens on two or more of these flows simultaneously. The result of such a change is that the resulting execution is *sequential* but *indeterminate in order*. In Figure 9.7, the transformation is enabled simultaneously with the arrival of an instance of Aircraft Number. The result is that *either* the Enable *or* the arrival of Aircraft Number is interpreted as having happened first and that it is indeterminate whether or not the transformation has produced an output.

Now that the preliminaries have been disposed of, let's examine the first of the three levels of execution.

9.5 Schematic execution of a transformation schema

The purpose of schematic execution is to show that the overall *pattern* of the system model is correct – that the system will produce the correct outputs in qualitative terms given a pattern of inputs. In this type of execution, tokens are not associated with values of flows. In order to be schematically executed, a transformation schema must obey the conventions for separation of data and control transformations, must obey all mechanical consistency rules, and must have a state-transition diagram (or an equivalent representation) associated with each of its control transformations. Furthermore, all data transformations with discrete data inputs must be synchronous, as defined in Chapter 6. In order to prepare the schema for execution, the following steps are taken:

- Tokens are placed on all time-continuous data flows that are inputs to the schema.

- Tokens are placed on data transformations with no prompts; these are considered permanently enabled.

- All unprompted control transformations are placed in their initial states.

- Tokens are placed on output event flows of control transformations as required by the initial states.

- Any executions required by the previous steps are performed; in other words, the initial state of a system might require a data transformation to be enabled and to be producing values of a continuous output.

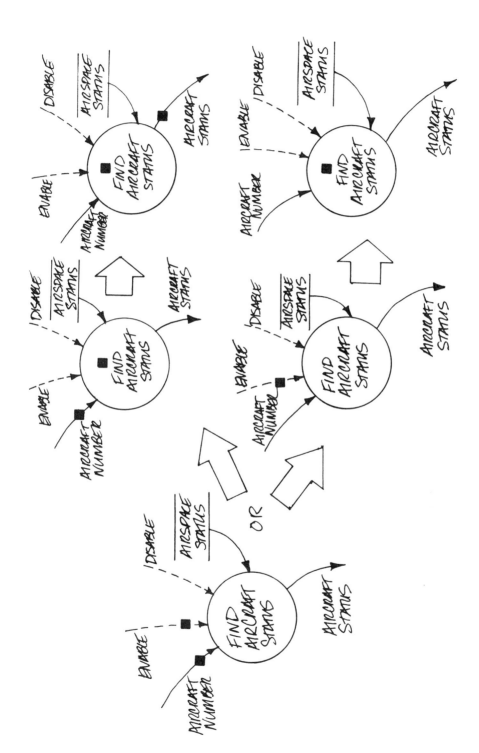

Figure 9.7. Results of simultaneous token placement.

● A token or tokens are placed in any control store with an initial value greater than zero.

Figure 9.8 shows a simple transformation schema that is prepared for execution.

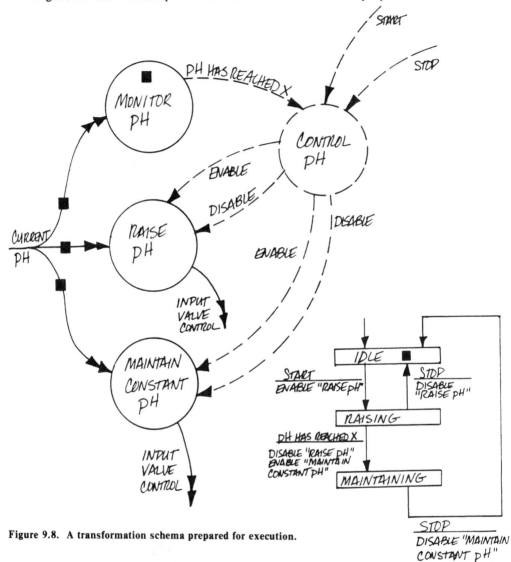

Figure 9.8. A transformation schema prepared for execution.

The execution plan is called a *scenario* and consists of a number of steps. Each step consists of a description of the real-world situation being simulated and a statement of the required token placement. Tokens may be placed on input flows to the schema. Tokens may also be placed on output event flows from data transformations; this placement simulates the occurrence of whatever the transformation was checking for. A sample scenario to be applied to Figure 9.8 is shown in Table 9.2. To carry out each step of the scenario, the following must happen: Tokens are placed. The schema is executed; this may require more than one cycle, since execution of one transformation may force execution of another. Any output tokens that have been placed on discrete outputs of the schema are recorded and removed.

TABLE 9.2 - A SIMPLE·SCENARIO		
STEP	SITUATION	TOKEN PLACEMENT
1	SYSTEM IS STARTED UP	ADD TOKEN TO "START" FLOW
2	pH REACHES DESIRED VALUE	ADD TOKEN TO "pH HAS REACHED X" FLOW

Table 9.2. A simple scenario.

When the first step of the scenario in Table 9.2 is applied to Figure 9.8, there are two cycles of execution. In the first cycle, the placement of the token on the Start flow changes the state to Raising and causes a token to be placed on the Enable flow to Raise pH. The second cycle is caused by the enabling of Raise pH, and causes the transformation to begin producing values of Input Valve Control. The results of executing the first step of the scenario are shown in Figure 9.9. We invite the reader to work out the next step as an exercise.

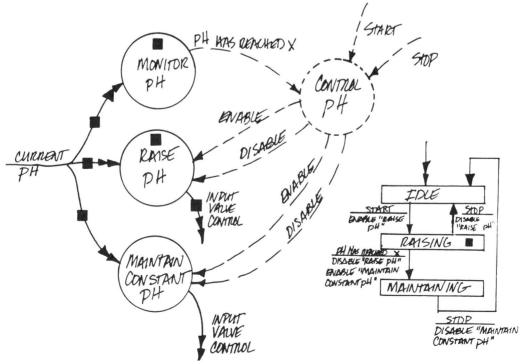

Figure 9.9. Results of schematic execution.

It is important to note the effect of schematic execution on a data transformation that has more than one discrete output. Figure 9.10 is a more realistic version of the transformation introduced in Figure 9.1. Under symbolic execution, this transformation will produce one of its discrete outputs; however, which one is produced is indeterminate. The indeterminacy can be removed by modifying the scenario so that it specifies the production of a specific output of such a transformation, rather than simply the arrival of an input.

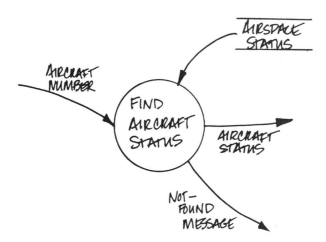

Figure 9.10. Data transformation with alternative outputs.

Now let's look at a more elaborate way of executing a schema.

9.6 Prototype execution of a transformation schema

Prototype execution, in addition to simulating the qualitative aspects of the system being modeled, simulates its quantitative aspects. The results of the prototype execution show not only which outputs are produced, but also what their values are. A schema that is executed in paper-and-pencil fashion by a group of developers qualifies as a prototype, although the term is more commonly applied to an automated simulation of the system's operation.

The intention of prototyping a schema is not to create an implementation of the schema but to understand the requirement embodied in it. A set of test cases comprising various input values is applied, and the outputs are examined. An unacceptable output value (assuming it doesn't simply reflect a construction error) is a symptom of a poorly defined requirement or a misunderstanding of the nature of the transformation work to be carried out by the schema. Such information may be used incidently to modify the prototype but it is used more importantly to clarify understanding of the requirements.

In addition to the preconditions for schematic execution, prototype execution imposes two other requirements. First, each data transformation within the data schema must have an associated transformation specification. Second, the initial values of the stored data within the schema and of the continuous data inputs must be specified prior to performing the execution. There is, however, one requirement for schematic execution that no longer applies. If the transformation specification defines the handling of asynchronous arrival of input flows, a transformation may have two or more discrete inputs.

The required form of the transformation specifications depends on the nature of the execution to be performed. If execution is to be done manually, any specification that is unambiguously interpretable is satisfactory. If an automated execution is desired, the transformation specifications must be written in a high-level language that can be executed on a development machine. The required form of initial value specifications also depends on the nature of the execution. In the manual case, a paper-and-pencil list of data elements with initial values will suffice. For automated execution, an actual database corresponding to the stored data layout of the transformation schema must be defined and loaded. Furthermore, the database must be accessible from the language in which the transformation specifications are written.

In the case of an automated prototype, flows from one transformation to another will need to be simulated by a task communication or subroutining facility. Since implementation timing constraints need not be met, a multi-tasking execution environment is not necessary. Potentially concurrent transformations can be "serialized" — executed one at a time in an arbitrary sequence.

Not only are the preconditions and support requirements for prototype execution more elaborate, but there are also additional requirements on the scenario. These requirements apply to both discrete data inputs and continuous data inputs. In any step in the scenario in which the occurrence of a discrete data input is simulated, the values of all associated data elements must be specified. In the case of continuous data inputs, the scenario must provide a means of determining input values at times following the start of the scenario. In the case of a monitored input, specifying input values at various points in time may suffice, with the input assumed to vary smoothly in the intervals between the points. However, if closed-loop control is to be realistically simulated, a formula for determining input values as a function of values of the controlling output must normally be given. In other words, a transformation specification for the *controlled* portion of the loop must be provided.

9.7 Direct implementation of a transformation schema

In principle, the transformation schema, together with its data and transformation specifications, could be compiled into executable code and implemented like any other program. Many of the required software support facilities exist in currently available languages. Ada, for example, provides task communication and co-ordination facilities that can implement the flow of data and control among transformations (see Booch [2]).

Unfortunately, at the time of writing, there is no graphic compiler for transformation schemas with an embedded specification language. Although practical methods for schematic and prototype execution can be pieced together from available software tools, the direct translation of a model of this kind into an implementation is an unrealized goal.

9.8 Summary

Execution of a transformation schema formalizes and adds rigor to the task of ensuring the adequacy of a system model. The rules for execution, coupled with the availability of automated tools, can reduce or even eliminate the distinction between requirements modeling and requirements prototyping.

Chapter 9: References

1. J.L. Peterson, Petri Nets. *Computing Surveys,* Vol. 9, No. 3, Sept. 1977.

2. G. Booch. *Software Engineering with Ada* (Menlo Park: Benjamin/Cummings Publishing Company, Inc., 1983), p. 234.

10

Modeling Stored Data

10.1 Introduction

The *data schema* models a system as a passive entity – as a network of categories that are linked to one another by their associations. In this chapter, we will introduce the notation for the data schema, give some illustrations of how the schema can be used, and introduce rules for judging whether a data schema is internally consistent and whether it communicates clearly. The data schema uses the basic notation and concepts of the *entity-relationship diagram* introduced by Chen [1], with some extensions to the notation and some refinement rules proposed by Flavin [2]. We believe that the model described in this chapter substantially meets the criteria for an adequate semantic data model proposed by Schrefl, Toa, and Wagner [3].

10.2 Basic notation: object types and relationships

The data schema as a descriptive tool is a graphics-oriented abstraction on the use of nouns and verbs in spoken or written language. Figure 10.1 is a data schema based on the sentence "Aircraft land on runways." By using a noun we *objectify* something – we make it into a "thing" -- which can then be manipulated by comparison with or differentiation from other things. The *object type,* shown by a box with a name in it, represents a set of real-world entities that play a role in a system. The word "type" is added to "object" to emphasize that a collection rather than an individual instance is represented.

We use verbs in sentences to describe linkages between nouns. Object types are similarly connected by *relationships,* shown by diamonds with names in them. The relationship represents a trace of a particular kind of interaction amoung the object types it connects. A relationship is inherently multidirectional, although limitations on names often mean that a relationship "reads" better in one direction or another. In the case of Figure 10.1, "Runways are landed on by aircraft" and "Aircraft land on runways" are equally legitimate.

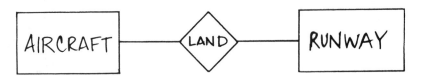

Figure 10.1. A simple data schema.

Although the point may seem obvious, it's important to differentiate object types from the real-world entities that they represent. By attaching a name to an entity or a collection of entities, we commit ourselves to dealing with it from a certain point of view. By naming something an "aircraft" rather than a "metal structure," we put it in the same category as certain wooden structures (gliders) that can also fly through the air and land on runways, and in a different category from other metal structures (hangars) that can't fly but in which things can be stored. The object type Aircraft is thus inevitably associated with a certain role, and it's the role that defines the "sameness" of the entities that we name "aircraft." The fact that there's only one instance of something doesn't disqualify it as an object type — it just so happens that only one entity plays that role in a particular system.

Just as an object type can represent more than one real-world entity, a relationship can represent more than one association. In Figure 10.1, the relationship Land stands for the set of associations between many different individual aircraft and runways. The diamond representing the relationship is named because it represents a specific type of linkage; aircraft also take off from runways, but that's a different association between the same two object types.

Figure 10.2 shows a more elaborate data schema that illustrates some other features of the basic notation. The Land and Take Off relationships reiterate the point that two or more different associations may exist among the same object types. An object type may be related to more than one other object type; Aircraft is related to Runway, Passenger, and Pilot. Furthermore, three or more object types may be associated by a relationship; Fly connects Pilot, Aircraft, and Passenger. At the other extreme, a relationship may have connections to only one object type; the fact that two runways intersect is represented by a linkage of two instances of the same object type. Finally, an object type need not represent a physical object. Although a Flight Plan may be thought of as typed on a sheet of paper, it's no less a flight plan if communicated orally or stored as an energy pattern in computer memory.

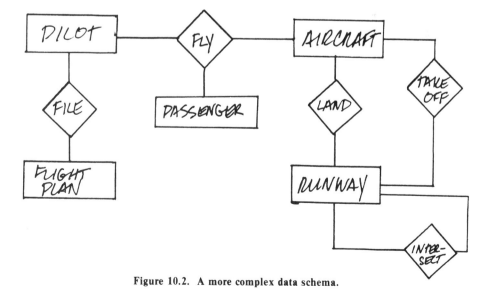

Figure 10.2. A more complex data schema.

10.3 Object types as stored data categories

The model we have just described can be used in a very general way to model the semantics of some subject area. Used in this way, it is better thought of as the schematic portion of an *information model*. It can help clarify thinking about a subject by laying out the relevant categories of knowledge and their associations — a use that may have nothing to do with a systems-development project. By choosing the name "data schema" to describe our model, we have declared our intention to think of object types as data storage categories. An object type is thus an abstraction from the various mechanisms for data storage — files, data bases, buffers, stacks, queues, common areas -- used in automated or manual systems. This use does not conflict with the broader interpretation of the model, since knowledge categories can be used to organize a collection of data items. It simply reflects our more specialized needs.

10.4 Comparison of transformation and data schemas

Our teaching experience has led us to conclude that many systems developers have difficulty understanding data schemas and similar types of models. We believe that this is a result of a deeply ingrained and quite natural bias toward models that represent things happening. Both traditional systems development tools such as flow charts and newer tools like transformation schemas can be pictured as showing systems in action, carrying out processes and transformations of inputs into outputs. A data schema is not an active model; it represents associations among categories about which data is kept. A library cataloging scheme is a good analogy to a data schema, as shown in Figure 10.3. The library's catalogue contains facts about authors, facts about fiction books, and facts about non-fiction books. Connections among categories are the result of the fact that certain authors have written certain books; the connections could be represented by cross-referencing within the cataloging scheme.

A potential area of confusion in interpreting data schemas is the use of active verbs (like "Write" in Figure 10.3) to name relationships. The relationship does *not* describe the act of writing. It represents the set of associations between particular authors and particular books that are the result or trace of the act of writing. As another example, consider the relationship "connect" between a distillation column and a supply tank in a refinery. The relationship describes not the act of laying the supply line to form the connection, but the structural relationship between the tank and the column that resulted.

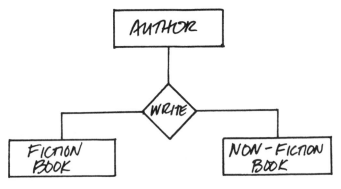

Figure 10.3. Data schema for a library.

Another potential source of confusion is the redundancy between the transformation schema and the data schema. Names that appear on object types and relationships will also appear on stores in the transformation schema (Figure 10.4). This overlap is caused by the transformation schema's description of the use of stored data by transformations. In fact, since the transformation specifications must contain descriptions of the formation or use of connections among stores, all the information on the data schema can be packaged within the transformation schema. Nevertheless, we recommend the creation of a data schema whenever there are non-trivial requirements for data-storage within a system. One reason is that the information about stored-data categories and associations, if contained only in the transformation schema and its associated specifications, is mixed in with transformation details. Since the purpose of system modeling is to allow visualization and verification of the system's connections, the data schema is required to provide the necessary illumination by highlighting the stored-data connections and allowing the model builder or reviewer to focus on them. Another reason for using a data schema is that the process of building a transformation schema provides no guidelines for partitioning data elements into stores. The model builder's choice to put all data into a single store, to create a multitude of simple stores, or to do something in between must be arbitrary or intuitive if the transformation schema alone is used. The building of a data schema offers refinement rules to assist in stored-data partitioning; the resultant partitioning can then be transferred to the transformation schema.

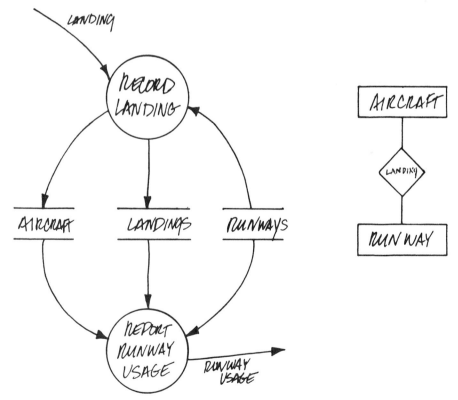

Figure 10.4. Overlap between transformation and data schema.

A final observation concerns the differing levels of susceptibility to change of transformation and data schemas. Figure 10.5 is an elaboration of Figure 10.4 in which there are now two sources of information about landings and two different requirements for retrieval of the stored data. Since the data arrives from different sources, it must be manipulated differently before storage (the radar data may be recorded only if a pilot's message was not received), and may be retrieved in different subsets and variously organized for output. The transformations have changed substantially. However, the stored data organization has changed little, if at all. Since the transformations are somewhat dependent on the connections to the system's environment, they are liable to change if the connections change. The data schema tends to depend more on the fundamental nature of the environment and is less vulnerable to change.

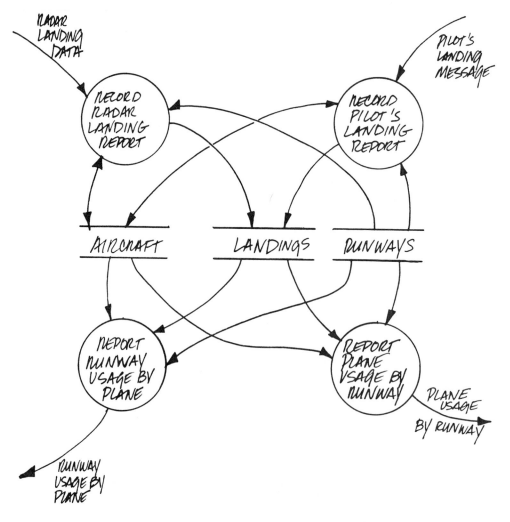

Figure 10.5. Multiple storage and retrieval transformations.

10.5 Advanced notation — classification of object types

The data schema becomes a more useful picture of a system's data organization if we differentiate various classes of object types. Let's begin by examining the role of the schema as an organization method for data elements. Since object types are subject-matter categories, a data element can be *attributed* to a particular object type. Picture yourself with a data element in hand, looking over a data schema, and placing the data element on the object type that it most closely describes. In Figure 10.2, Number of Engines is clearly attributable to Aircraft, and Runway Surface Material is attributable to Runway. Are there any data elements attributable to a relationship? Clearly there is some information involved with the occurrence of a relationship; for example, an instance of Land connects a specific occurrence of Runway with a specific occurrence of Aircraft. We could represent this information in terms of data elements by concatenating an aircraft number and a runway number. However, we will adopt the convention that the identification of the objects linked by a relationship is not represented in terms of data elements. (Think of the relationship information as inherent in the structure of the schema.) Even with the use of this convention there are unresolved issues. Consider the data elements Time of Landing, Wind Speed, and Wind Direction. Although it could be attributed to the Aircraft or to the Runway, Time of Landing describes the relationship between the two object types better than it describes either of them individually. To deal with this situation, we introduce the idea of the associative object type.

As illustrated by Figure 10.6, an associative object type is denoted by a relationship symbol with no label and by an object type symbol with an arrowhead pointing into the relationship whose name applies to both the object and to the relationship. The notation means that Landing plays a dual role in the model as follows: As a relationship, each occurrence of Landing links an instance of Aircraft with an instance of Runway and contains inherent structural information identifying the two instances. As an object type, each occurrence of Landing is described by the data elements and may be linked by other relationships to occurrences of other object types.

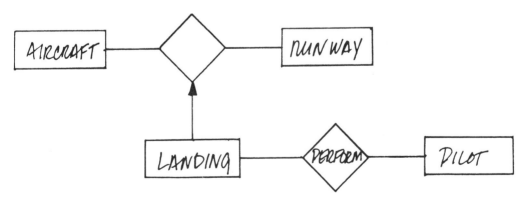

Figure 10.6. Data schema with associative object.

By changing the verb Land into the noun Landing, we have objectified it — we have identified a Landing as a "thing" that can be dealt with in the same way as other object types in the model. Just as we can speak of "The aircraft with number N234786 and two engines," we can speak of "The landing that occurred at 7:30 PM with a 35 mph wind from the east." However, the arrow indicates an important difference between Landing on the one hand and Aircraft and Runway on the other. There can be instances of (newly constructed) aircraft that have never landed on a runway, or of (newly constructed) runways on which aircraft have never landed. However, an instance of a Landing (excluding emergency landings) requires pre-existing instances of an Aircraft and a Runway. Associative object types are thus dependent on the existence of other object types; ordinary object types do not have this dependency.

Associative object types can act as relationships between several different object types. In Figure 10.6, only two object types are related through the associative object type, but it is possible to construct a diagram (such as Figure 10.7) in which there are three (or even more) object types. In this example, the Compilation object type, which describes data about a single compilation by a compiler of a source program into an object program, cannot exist without the prior existence of all three of the object types.

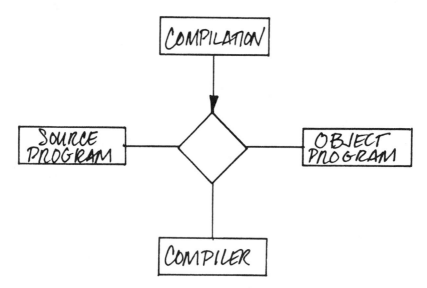

Figure 10.7. Associative object type and the object types it depends on.

Let's now examine another distinction between classes of object types: subtype/supertype object types. Bottle Filling Valve and Solution Tank are potential object types from a bottling system. The data element Valve Position is attributable to Bottle Filling Valve, and Tank Level can be attributed to Solution Tank. What about Time of Next Scheduled Inspection, which might be included in the system to prompt the operator? Either the tank or the valve could conceivably be inspected for accumulated residue and mechanical problems. This is a different situation from the one involving Time of Landing mentioned earlier in this section. Time of Landing applies jointly to the combination of Aircraft and Runway. Time of Next Scheduled Inspection could apply individually to either Bottle Filling Valve or Solution Tank. The data element really describes an object type that we can call Production Equipment and that has a broader membership than either Bottle Filling Valve or Solution Tank. A possible way of dealing with this situation is to replace the two previous object types with the single object type Production Equipment. This has the disadvantages that it hides the differences between the various types of equipment and that data elements such as Tank Level don't apply to all occurences of Production equipment. Another possibility is that both Bottle Filling Valve and Solution Tank might be described by Date of Next Scheduled Inspection. This has the disadvantage that the commonality between the two pieces of equipment is not represented. A better solution than either of the previous two is shown in Figure 10.8. A special subtype/supertype relationship connects Production Equipment with Bottle Filling Valve and Solution Tank. A crossbar on the line from one of the object types indicates that it is the supertype. As with associative object types, there are dependencies among subtype/supertype object types. Each instance of each of the object types must participate in exactly one occurrence of the relationship. Each subtype instance must be linked to a supertype instance, and each supertype instance must be linked to an instance of one of the subtypes. Another way to think about this is that a real-world instance of production equipment is represented in the model by a pair of object type instances, which between them contain the data about the equipment.

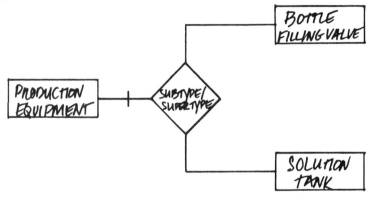

Figure 10.8. Subtype and supertype object types.

A final distinction among object types concerns the nature of the data elements attributed to an object type. Consider the following list of data elements that might describe Aircraft: Aircraft Number, Passenger Capacity, Engine Serial Number, Engine Horsepower. It is also possible to think of this list as containing three data elements that describe the Aircraft and two that describe the Engine. Engine can thus be raised to object-type status (Figure 10.9). A process like this one results in the creation of a *characteristic object type*. (There is no special notation.) Something that was depicted in terms of data elements about another object becomes an object in its own right. A possible characteristic object type exists whenever a group of data elements attributed to an object type consists of one element that identifies a different object type and other elements that describe that object type.

Figure 10.9. A characteristic object type.

The idea of characteristic object type implies that the distinction between an object type and a data element is only a relative one. It is useful to picture an object type as consisting of a group of characteristics to which it is bound by internal relationships (Figure 10.10). If the characteristic is of relatively minor importance in the system, it is represented by a single data element attributed to the object type and is invisible at the schematic level. If the characteristic is more important, it becomes objectified, it is described by a number of data elements, and its relationship to the original object becomes external and appears on the schema. This may occur at any level of description.

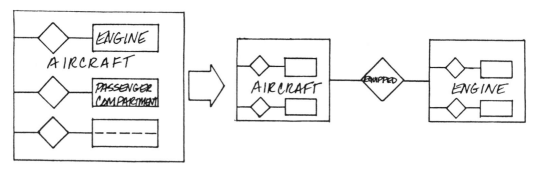

Figure 10.10. Characteristics as internal relationships.

Notice that all the preceding specialized object types have a relationship to an object type from which they were derived — the associative object type to the object types that it relates, the subtype to the supertype and vice versa, the characteristic to the "parent."

10.6 Connection rules

The rules for connecting the elements of a data schema are as follows: An object type must be connected to zero or more relationships. A relationship must be connected to one or more object types. An object type may not be directly connected to another object type. A relationship may not be directly connected to another relationship.

10.7 Internal consistency

The rules for data-schema consistency are drawn from the schema's role as specifying a data-classification scheme. This role requires that data must be able to be "put into" and "taken out of" the model unambiguously. In order for a data schema to be considered internally consistent, the following rules apply: Each object type must have a unique name. Each relationship must have a unique name. Each instance of each object type must be uniquely identifiable.* Each instance of each relationship must be uniquely identifiable.*

In addition to these basic consistency rules, there are some other useful guidelines for data-schema consistency. Strictly speaking, the overall correctness of a schema cannot be verified unless all object types and relationships are specified. However, many obvious errors can be detected by applying an informal understanding of the object types and relationships. In the case of the transformation schema, this was done by focusing on the flows and stores; in the present case it's done by focusing on the relationships.

Specifically, relationships should be eliminated from the data schema if they describe associations that do not or cannot exist within the subject matter — a Land relationship between Airport and Runway, for example. Relationships that are irrelevant to the system should also be removed. A Lives in Vicinity relationship between Pilot and Airport may exist but may be totally meaningless within the context of a particular system. Finally, a relationship should be removed if it is redundant; that is, if the association it describes is already described by some combination of other relationships. In Figure 10.11, we can ask, Does the Filled With relationship mean anything more than that a Solution Batch was fed through a Bottle Filling Valve and that the Bottle was filled by the valve? If the answer is no, the Filled With relationship is redundant. However, the answer may be yes — some other method of getting solution into bottles exists — and the relationship may in fact be necessary.

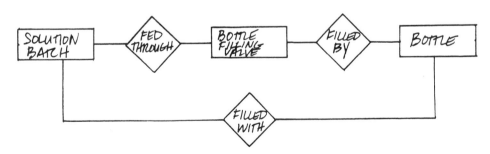

Figure 10.11. A potentially redundant relationship.

The preceding guidelines are related to the removal of relationships. To decide whether relationships need to be added to a data schema, it is useful to apply the idea of a question-answering machine. A data schema is internally coherent only if it can provide data as required. This means that whenever an item of required information contains data elements belonging to two or more object types, the object types must be directly or indirectly related in such a way that the item can be extracted. Referring to Figure 10.6, the data schema can be used to answer the following questions: Which air-

---

* This topic will be dealt with in more detail in Chapter 11, Specifying Data.

craft landed on a runway? Which runways has an aircraft landed on? Which landings has a pilot made? Which pilot made a particular landing? Which aircraft was a pilot flying during a particular landing? Which runway did a pilot use during a particular landing? Which aircraft have been landed by a pilot? Which runways have been used for landings by a pilot?

However, the schema cannot answer the question, What aircraft is a pilot qualified to fly? This would require an additional relationship, since a pilot may be qualified to fly an aircraft that he or she has never landed.

10.8 Semantic clarity rules

It is possible for a data schema to obey all the connection rules and internal consistency rules and still be unsatisfactory as a model. As with the transformation schema, the data schema is a human communication tool — it assists a person in visualizing a system and in communicating that visualization to other people. We must therefore subject data schemas to some guidelines to determine how useful they are in communicating meaning.

Consider the three (partial) schemas illustrated in Figure 10.12, in which an object type and some of the attributed data elements have been shown for each. Although each schema is drawn from the same general subject matter, the choice of object types has been made quite differently in each case. The Runway object (a) is drawn from a system whose subject matter is Airport Facilities Maintenance. Although Runway is an object type, aircraft and landings are of only subsidiary importance and are represented in summary fashion by data elements. The other object types in this system might include Hangar, Passenger Terminal, and so on. The other two examples in this figure reflect similarly specialized subject matters.

The lesson to be drawn from Figure 10.12 is that the choice of object types is linked with the relative importance to the system of various aspects of the system's environment. Semantic clarity will be lost if unimportant aspects are elevated to object type status. If, for instance, Aircraft were chosen as an object type in example (a) from Figure 10.12, a distinction of relatively minor significance (particular aircraft as sources of wear and tear on a runway) would be overemphasized. Semantic clarity will also be lost if important distinctions are not elevated to object-type status. In the example, choosing Thing to be Maintained rather than Runway, Hangar, and so on, as an object type would suppress the important ways in which maintaining runways differs from maintaining hangars or terminal buildings.

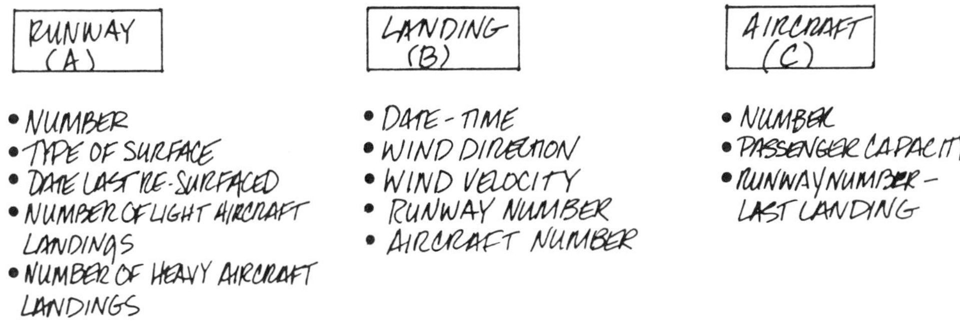

RUNWAY
(A)

- NUMBER
- TYPE OF SURFACE
- DATE LAST RE-SURFACED
- NUMBER OF LIGHT AIRCRAFT LANDINGS
- NUMBER OF HEAVY AIRCRAFT LANDINGS

LANDING
(B)

- DATE-TIME
- WIND DIRECTION
- WIND VELOCITY
- RUNWAY NUMBER
- AIRCRAFT NUMBER

AIRCRAFT
(C)

- NUMBER
- PASSENGER CAPACITY
- RUNWAY NUMBER - LAST LANDING

Figure 10.12. Variants on a data schema.

Another criterion for object-type refinement is to examine the data elements that describe the object type. If there are no data elements other than elements that make up the identifier for each occurrence of the object, then the object type may be removed. Other object types that participate in a relationship with the removed object type should be extended to include data elements that describe the removed object type. Data elements that don't apply to all instances of an object type suggest that the object type should be expanded into a supertype and subtypes. Data elements that seem to apply jointly to a combination of object types suggest a missing associative object type. Data elements that seem to apply individually to two or more object types suggest a missing supertype object type.

Please refer back to the discussion in section 10.5 of this chapter for more details.

After refinement of object types, it is possible to have an associative object type that is related to only one object type. Figure 10.13 shows a fragment of a data schema that stores data about flights that an aircraft has made. Included in the Flight object type is data about the Pilot that flew the plane. In this model, the flight cannot have been made without a pilot. The diagram was derived from Figure 10.14; however, the Pilot object type had insufficient significance to warrant retaining it as an object type, and it was removed.

Relationships in a data schema provide important clues as to whether the object types have the appropriate level of generality. In Figure 10.15, the relationship Maintain is more of an association between the Engine Mechanic and the Engine than between the Engine Mechanic and the Aircraft. The relationship is too general, suggesting that Aircraft may be concealing a potentially significant, more specific object type. The solution is to elevate Engine to the status of a characteristic object type. In Figure 10.16, a similar real-world situation leads to a conclusion in the opposite direction. If the operator's inspection of the valve and the tank doesn't differ much (refer to the discussion of figure 10.7), the two Inspect relationships are too specific. This suggests there should be a single relationship to an object type that emphasizes the similarities of valves and tanks; in other words, a supertype object type.

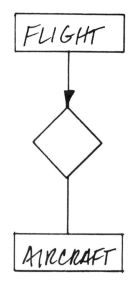

Figure 10.13. Associative object type with only one remaining connection.

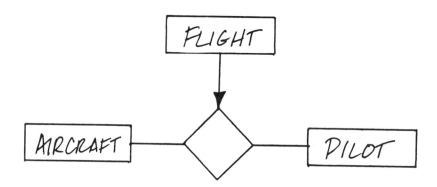

Figure 10.14. Entity-relationship diagram prior to removal of object type.

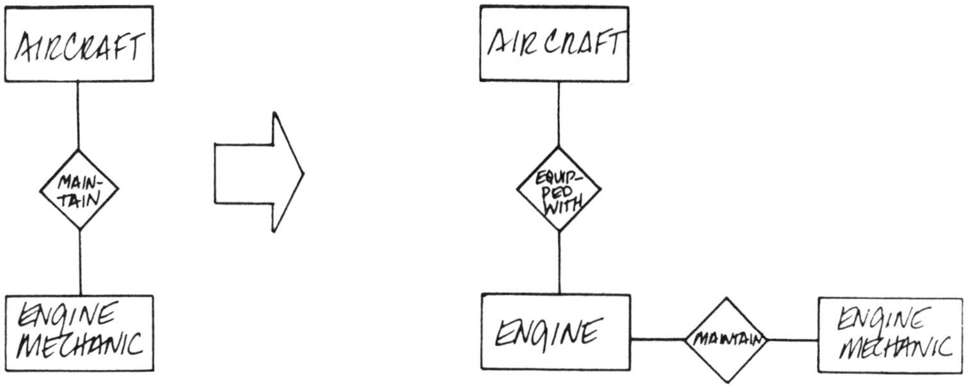

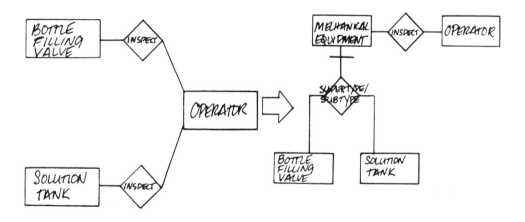

Figure 10.15.   Refinement triggered by over-general relationship.

Figure 10.16.   Refinement triggered by over-specific relationship.

10.9 Summary

The data schema is a tool used as an adjunct to the transformation schema to describe the stored data layout of a system. We have focused on describing categories of stored data and the relationships between them. As we stated in section 10.3, the schema can also be used as a general semantic model in which object types and relationships are modeled, whether or not data is stored about the object type or the association. We have chosen to describe the more restricted form of model.

The data schema is incomplete without a precise description of both the object type and the relationships. These issues are covered in the next chapter, Specifying Data.

Chapter 10: References

1. P.P. Chen. "The Entity-Relationship Model — Toward a Unified View of Data," *ACM Transactions on Database Systems,* Vol 1, No. 1 (March 1976), pp. 9-36

2. M. Flavin. *Fundamental Concepts of Information Modeling* (New York, Yourdon Press, 1981).

3. M. Schrefl, A.M. Tjoa, and R.R. Wagner. "Comparision Criteria for Semantic Data Models," *Proceedings, IEEE Data Engineering Conference,* Los Angeles, 1984.

11
Specifying Data

11.1 Introduction

The flows and stores on the transformation schema and the object types and relationships on the data schema declare components that must be specified precisely. These components can all be regarded as *data items,* although they appear in several different forms on the two schemas. We must now address the problem of the specification of these components, so that we can produce a rigorous model.

Before we plunge into the details of these specifications, let us first establish a framework for the major issues that need to be addressed. Data has three aspects — meaning, composition and type — that are commonly confused. To get a clear picture of data we need to think about each aspect separately; each of the next three sections deals with one of these aspects. A notation is then defined for specifying each aspect. Finally, the specifications are related back to the schemas.

11.2 Specifying meaning

The following discussion between Humpty Dumpty and Alice, taken from Carroll's *Through the Looking Glass* is illustrative of what we intend when we talk about the meaning of data:

"I don't know what you mean by 'glory'," Alice said.

Humpty Dumpty smiled contemptuously. "Of course you don't — till I tell you. I meant 'there's a nice knock-down argument for you!' "

"But 'glory' doesn't mean 'a nice knock-down argument,'" ' Alice objected.

"When I use a word," Humpty Dumpty said, "it means just what I choose it to mean — neither more nor less."

The problem, of course, is that as soon as we *name* something, we all have to agree on what that name represents. Unfortunately, the way we describe the meaning of a word is by using still more words. In this sense, specifying the meaning of a data item used within a system is the same as defining a word in a natural-language dictionary, and it suffers from the same problems.

We specify the meaning of a data item by stating the role that the thing referred to by the data item plays in the system. For example, we could define Aircraft Position as a measure of the position of an aircraft relative to the center of the Earth. The meaning of the data item does not uniquely specify the composition of the data that is used to represent it. Aircraft Position could be represented by latitude, longitude, and height or by a Cartesian representation using the center of the Earth as origin. Meanings are often stated in terms of composition. For example, "AIRCRAFT POSITION is the latitude, longitude, and height of the aircraft." This type of definition confuses the composition of data with its interpretation and is often unnecessarily narrow in scope.

11.3 Specifying composition

A data item declared on one of the schemas may be either elemental or composite. A composite data item is one that is composed of other data items (which may, in turn, also be composite), and an elemental data item is one that cannot be decomposed further. Using the Aircraft Position example, we can specify that Aircraft Position is a composite of latitude, longitude, and height. In contrast, latitude, longitude, and height are elemental and have no compositions.

A data composition specification states the names and relationships of the data items, that, when taken together, play the role defined by the meaning specification. In other words, when we define the composition of a data item, we are defining which data items are used to make it up.

11.4 Specifying type

Elemental data items, or *data elements,* may take on values, and, by extension, the value of a composite data item is a composite of these values. For modeling purposes, the actual value of a data element at a point in time is irrelevant; we are concerned only with the *set* of values that the data element can take on. We shall use the word "type" to identify this characteristic of a data element. (The words "domain" or "range" are often used in this connection.)

Our use of the word "type" is consistent with its use in programming-language theory. However, in practice the word is often associated with the physical representation of the data. This is particularly true for FORTRAN where only two types are defined (INTEGER and REAL) and all other data types must be mapped into one or the other. If we were implementing a card-playing program in FORTRAN, we might have to represent the value of a single card as a pair of integers — the first between 1 and 4, the second between 1 and 13.

In reality, we don't care about these numeric values; we are interested only in the suit and the face values. The value representation of the ace of spades is much clearer as "Ace, Spades" than as "13,4." Modern programming languages such as Ada permit the definition of such extended data types, along with redefinition of operations to permit correct computation on values, so that it is possible to add 1 to "10" and get the result J. Our use of "type" should be thought of in this more general sense.

Some data elements may take on continuous ranges of values, or a large number of values for which enumeration is not useful. Such data elements may be specified by listing upper and lower limits on values, and precision, where relevant. We also consider units as part of the type definition. For example, Longitude could be specified with limits of 0 and 90, precision of 0.01, and units of degrees.

11.5 Notation for specifying meaning

Meaning is most clearly specified using natural language. Our notation for meaning, following DeMarco [1], places the data item specified on the left, followed by an equals symbol, followed by the meaning set off by asterisks. For example:

Aircraft Position = *measure of distance of aircraft from center
of earth*

11.6 Notation for specifying data composition

We shall use a somewhat modified version of the notation of DeMarco [2] for specifying the composition of data. The notation is based on the observation that, as with programs, all data compositions can be defined from a few basic constructions: composition, selection, and iteration. Table 11.1 lists the symbols and how they are read.

SYMBOL	READ AS
=	IS COMPOSED OF
+	TOGETHER WITH
[..|...|..]	SELECT ONE OF
{ ... }	ITERATIONS OF

Table 11.1. Data composition notation.

The equals symbol is used for introducing the composition of a named item. For example:

Aircraft Position = Latitude + Longitude + Height

The name on the left *is composed of* the items on the right. The composition on the right of the equals symbol may be arbitrarily complex, being made up of names and any of the three other symbols.

The plus symbol is used to denote concatenation. The symbol is read "together with" and has no connection with either the mathematical addition operator or the Boolean "or" symbol. No order is implied.

Selection is described by listing each item that may be chosen between square brackets, separated by vertical bars. So if we were to define State Display Request as follows:

$$\text{State Display Request} = [\text{Advance Request} \,|\, \text{Backup Request}]$$

this would say that a State Display request is *just one of* an Advance Request or a Backup Request. Any number of items may be specified, separated by vertical bars.

The braces { and } are used to denote iteration, so the entry

$$\text{Logic state} = \{\text{channel level}\}$$

defines a logic state to be a collection of channel levels. It is often useful to specify limits of iteration, thus:

$$\text{Logic state} = 4 \,\{\text{channel level}\}\, 10$$

which states that there must be at least four but no more than ten occurrences of the iterated construct. By default, if the lower bound is missing, the assumed minimum is zero, and if the upper bound is missing, there is no upper limit.

The notation may be nested to express more complex data structure. The expression

$$A = [\,\{\,C\,\}\,|\,X + Y\,]$$

indicates that an A consists of either a variable number of C's, or an X followed by a Y. Composition entries may also be arranged hierarchically by the use of intermediate data items. The set of composition entries

$$A = [\,Q\,|\,R\,]$$
$$Q = \{\,C\,\}$$
$$R = X + Y$$

is equivalent to the previous entry.

The DeMarco notation also uses parentheses to denote the optional presence of a data item within a composite. This notation is redundant, since the two expressions

$$X = Y + (\,Z\,)$$
$$X = Y + 0\{\,Z\,\}1$$

are equivalent.

In addition to the DeMarco notation, there are other notations that express data composition graphically. Jackson [3] uses boxes for named data structures with connectors to show composition. The connectors are annotated to show selection and iteration (see Figure 11.1). Orr [4] uses a bracket notation to express composition. Composition may also be expressed using the declaration capabilities of a high-level language.

11.7 Notation for specifying types

Every data element requires a type specification. As we indicated earlier, we shall restrict our use of the word "type" to specify the values and the units of each data element. All type specifications are delimited by asterisks . Type may be specified by any combination of enumeration, range, precision, and units.

We specify by enumeration using a notation similar to that for selection in a data composition specification, except that *[instead of [is used as a delimiter. For example:

Suit = *[Clubs | Diamonds | Hearts | Spades]*

should be read as, Suit may take the value Clubs, Diamonds, Hearts, or Spades. Suit is not *composed* of these values; the data item may simply take on these values.

A *range* may be specified by mapping the variable onto a previously defined range and by specifying limits where appropriate. Thus:

acceleration = *range:real*

which is a range with no limits; or

speed = *range:real, limits 0-100*

which defines a limited range.

Finally, precision or units may be included in a data element specification. For example:

speed = *range:real, limits 0-100, precision 0.01, units kph*

Since an event flow has no content, its type specification is unnecessary.

As with composition specifications, type specifications may also be expressed using the features of an appropriate high-level language, such as Pascal or Ada.

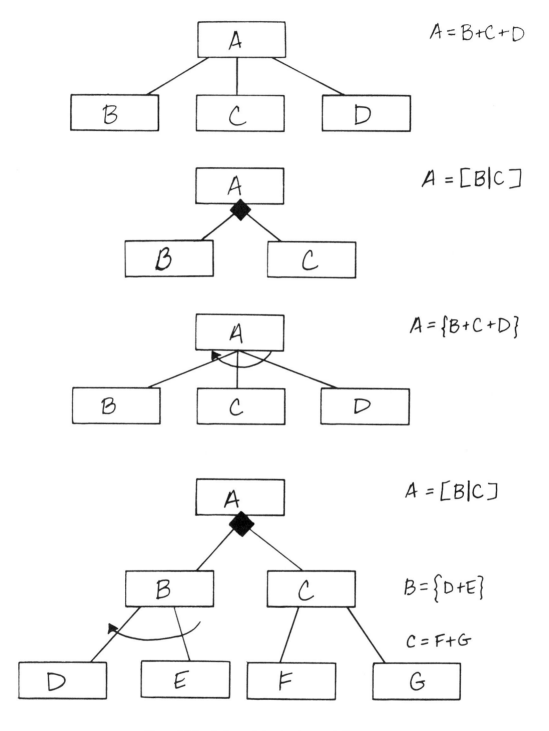

Figure 11.1. Jackson data structure notation.

11.8 Specifying components on the transformation schema

All flows and stores on the transformation schema need data specifications. Meaning must be specified for both flows and stores. Composite data flows and composite stores require data composition specifications. Data elements contained within flows and stores, elemental data flows, and elemental stores, all require a type specification. Data specifications for stores will be discussed further in the next section.

11.9 Specifying object types

All object types on a data schema require both meaning specifications and composition specifications.

Object types on a data schema and stores on a transformation schema both represent stored-data categories. A data specification can thus serve to specify both an object type and the corresponding store. Since stored-data categories typically represent collections of similar real-world entities, it is often necessary to name both the single occurrence of an entity and the set of entities. We will use the following conventions: The object type carries the name of the single occurrence. The store carries the name of the set of occurrences. The meaning specification is given under the name of the single occurrence. The composition specification for the set is in terms of an iteration of the single occurrence.

Consider the stored data representation of a set of circuit breakers. The data store would be called Breakers, and the object type would be called Breaker. The data specifications would be:

> Breakers = {Breaker}
> Breaker = *A switching device that controls the flow of current
>   through an electrical system*
>
> = @Breaker Id + Breaker Indication + Breaker Control

In Chapter 10, Modeling Stored Data, we indicated that each occurrence contained in a store or object type must be uniquely identifiable. This is required so that we can *unambiguously* access data about a single occurrence. The choice of the data element or set of data elements whose values are guaranteed to be unique for each occurrence should be indicated in the data specification. Each data element that makes up the identifier is prefaced with the symbol @, as illustrated in the composition specification for Breaker shown above. The identifier of an object type is indicated only in the composition specification.

Composition specifications for associative object types that depend on unique occurrences of other object types do not include their identifying data elements. Instead, the suffix "-ref" is added to the object type name to indicate a connection to an occurrence of the object type, regardless of the current data elements used to identify it[5]. For example, the associative object type Flight in Figure 11.2 would contain a composition specification as follows:

> Flight = @Aircraft-ref + @Pilot-ref + Time-of-departure +
>   Time-of-arrival

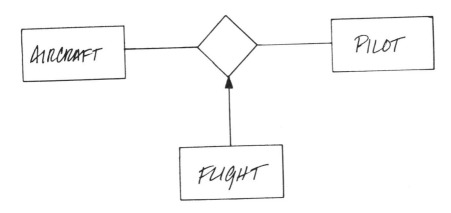

Figure 11.2. Object types to be specified.

Subtype/supertype object types require additional notation. Consider Figure 11.3: when we are thinking about a single occurrence of the supertype, we are choosing between different subtypes and including the data held in the supertype. We model this as follows:

Machine = *Common data: Date-of-maintenance + Engineer-name*
Machine = [Packing-machine | Spinning-machine]

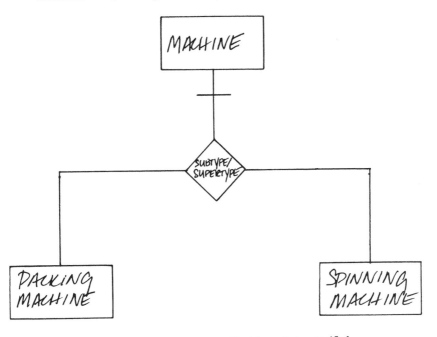

Figure 11.3. Subtype/supertype object types to be specified.

Note that the common data between the subtypes is included as a comment.

Conversely, when we think about the entire set of occurrences, we wish to model the subtypes together, thus:

Machines = {Packing-machines + Spinning-machines}

11.10 Specifying relationships

All relationships on a data schema require both meaning and composition specifications. As with object types, relationships may have corresponding data stores, and the same naming conventions apply.

The composition entry for a relationship must include references to object types linked by the relationship and an indication of the upper and lower limits on the number of occurrences that can participate in the relationship, using the iteration construction. For example, the relationship shown in Figure 11.4 may be described as:

Flight-qualifications = {Able-to-fly}
Able-to-fly = *Associates a pilot with all the types of
        aircraft he/she is qualified to fly*
    = Pilot-ref + 1 {Aircraft-type-ref}

Figure 11.4. Relationship to be specified.

It is also possible to define Able-to-fly as associating one pilot and one aircraft type.

Able-to-fly = Pilot-ref + Aircraft-type-ref

In this case there is a larger set of one-to-one occurrences, rather than a smaller set of one-to-many occurrences.

11.11 Summary

Each data name on both the schemas must be defined precisely in terms of its meaning, composition, and type. These data names include object types, data stores, flows, and relationships.

Chapter 11: References

1.   T. DeMarco. *Structured Analysis and System Specification* (New York: Yourdon Press, 1978), p.134.

2.   Ibid, p.133.

3.   M.A. Jackson. *Principles of Program Design* (New York: Academic Press, 1975).

4.   K. Orr. *Structured Systems Development* (New York: Yourdon Press, 1978)

5.   N. Matzke, S. Mellor, and P. Ward. Unpublished course notes for Yourdon, Inc's workshop entitled "Structured Analysis Workshop: Defining Requirements for Complex Systems."

12
Organizing the Model

12.1 Introduction

A system is modeled schematically by the data schema and transformation schema and then modeled precisely by detailed specifications of each component of the schemas. The detailed specifications, when related as shown by the schemas, are a complete representation of the system.

We now have enough of a conceptual framework to put together a model for a system of any size. However, for a system that is non-trivial, a single schematic transformation or data model would be too complex for convenient comprehension. Our problem, then, is to organize the model for the maximum convenience of the reader. This is far more than a "packaging" problem. The utility of a model as a vehicle for systems development depends on its verifiability, which in turn depends on its comprehensibility.

The problems we face when we try to communicate with other people are many and various. However, some themes recur, and as system developers we can extract some general guidelines. Please note that these are guidelines – not rules. The fundamental goal is communication; the means for achieving that goal are less important. *Complexity should be limited.*

Human beings can deal with only a small number of things at once. Each of us has suffered from overload at some time: too much information at once in a class, too many people speaking at once, too many things happening at once, or too many boxes and bubbles. This potential for overload is related to the number of things we can retain in our short-term memory. A paper by G.A. Miller [1] sets this number at seven plus or minus two. This is not the complete story, since we must also consider the interactions between the things remembered as a part of the complexity, but it does provide us with a guideline. *We should abide by communication protocols.* As we think about any problem, we tend to break it into sub-problems to avoid the complexity limit. Once a pattern of partitioning is wired in to the brain of a participant in a communication, it is extremely difficult to transmit information effectively using any other pattern. For example, when you next need to talk to a U.S. telephone operator, try supplying the required numbers in a pattern other than <area code> <exchange> <number>; say, in a 2-digit, 5-digit, 3-digit format. The confusion generated can be immense. The implication of this is that you must break down the material you wish to communicate in a way that is comfortable for the receiver.

The solution to the communication problem is to group the elements of a schema into larger units, according to the guidelines outlined above. But this introduces a new problem: how do we organize the resulting units?

12.2 Organizing a model hierarchically

We can represent a complex model as a hierarchy, as shown in Figure 12.1, where the lower rectangles spell out details that are summarized by the upper ones.

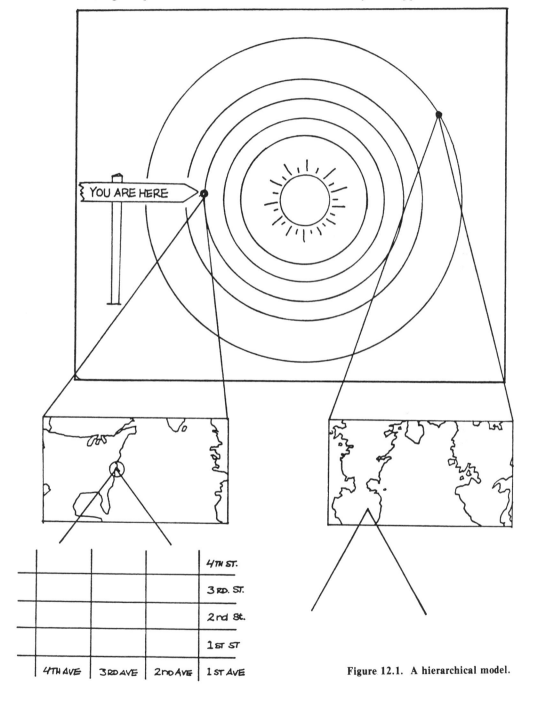

Figure 12.1. A hierarchical model.

Note that the packaging is an artifact that is superimposed on the the actual organization of the system and that adds no further information. The hierarchy we have imposed is one of representation only. Ideally, each rectangle will represent a portion of the model that contains just enough information to be comfortably assimilated. Since a video display screen often contains such a chunk of information, we will refer to the units of a hierarchical model as "screens."

The advantages of this type of representation are as follows: The complexity of each screen of the model is within human limits. The model is partitioned at multiple levels, allowing a reader to focus on only the part of the model of interest on a particular occasion.

The price we pay for these advantages is that we need to find a scheme for organizing the units of the hierarchical model and representing the interfaces between them. These problems are addressed in the following sections.

12.3 The concept of leveling

The notation of the transformation schema allows a single transformation, flow, or store to represent an arbitrarily large portion of a system. Consider the schema of Figure 12.2. It is possible to represent the same overall transformation pattern by a smaller number of transformations. In Figure 12.3, transformation G has subsumed transformations A, B, D, and F from Figure 12.2, and transformation H has subsumed transformations C and E. Figure 12.3 summarizes Figure 12.2 by suppressing some of its details. Transformations G and H constitute a *higher-level* representation of the system than the set of transformations A through F. Representing a group of transformations by a single higher-level transformation is referred to as *upward leveling*. Representing a higher-level transformation by a group of lower-level transformations is called *downward leveling*.

Flows and stores may be leveled as well as transformations. Figure 12.4 represents the same system as Figure 12.3, with flows M and L subsumed into flow I, flows Q and T subsumed into flow K, and stores R and S subsumed into store J.

Let's now look at an alternative organization of the system modeled in Figures 12.2 through 12.4. This organization is based on DeMarco [2].

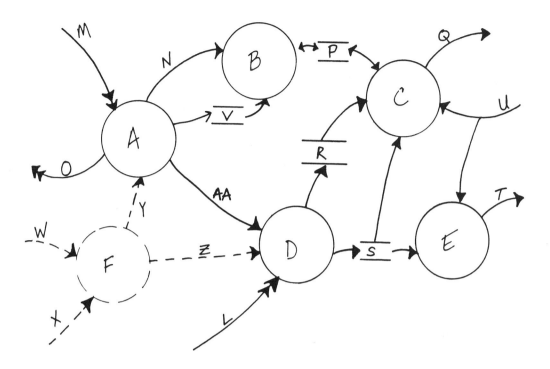

Figure 12.2. A transformation schema.

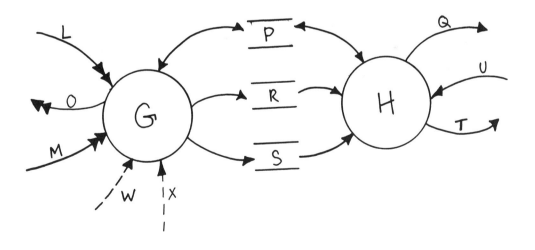

Figure 12.3. A transformation schema with leveled processes.

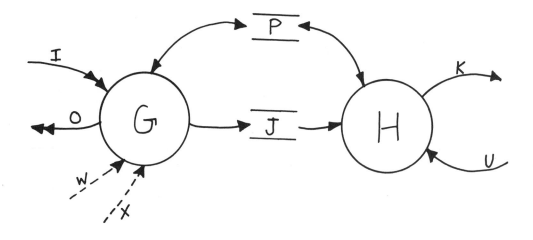

Figure 12.4. A transformation schema with leveled processes, flows, and stores.

12.4 The leveled transformation model

Figure 12.5 is a leveled set of transformation schemas. Each upper-level screen is a schema that summarizes the details of a set of lower-level schemas.

The schema at the top covers the whole system — but it is only a high-level view with few details. This highest level of the model is called the *context schema*. The context schema contains a single transformation representing the entire system. It also shows the interfaces between the system and the environment. In addition, the context schema shows the sources and destinations of flows that enter and leave the system. These *terminators* are represented by boxes and represent other systems, devices, or people that interact with the system being modeled. Terminators may be thought of as outside the scope of the system under study. The name on the context schema's single transformation describes the whole system and is also the name of a screen that contains the breakdown of the system into its major sub-systems. This next screen contains a number of transformations, whose names are, in turn, the names of succeeding screens. This leveling process may be continued for as many levels as is necessary to encompass the complexity of the system being modeled.

All the schemas in the leveled set, except for the context schema, contain flows with unspecified sources or destinations. For example, the screen labeled "Figure 2 — H" on Figure 12.5 does not show the source of flow U or the destination of flows Q and T. The absence of sources and destinations serves to reduce the complexity of the individual schemas. No information is lost, since the source or destination of any flow can be found on either the next-higher-level screen or on one of the screens above.

The conventions for the transformation schema permit flows between stores and transformations to be unnamed. To preserve the identity of stored-data interfaces, it is thus necessary to show a store at the highest level at which it connects two or more transformations and at all the levels below.

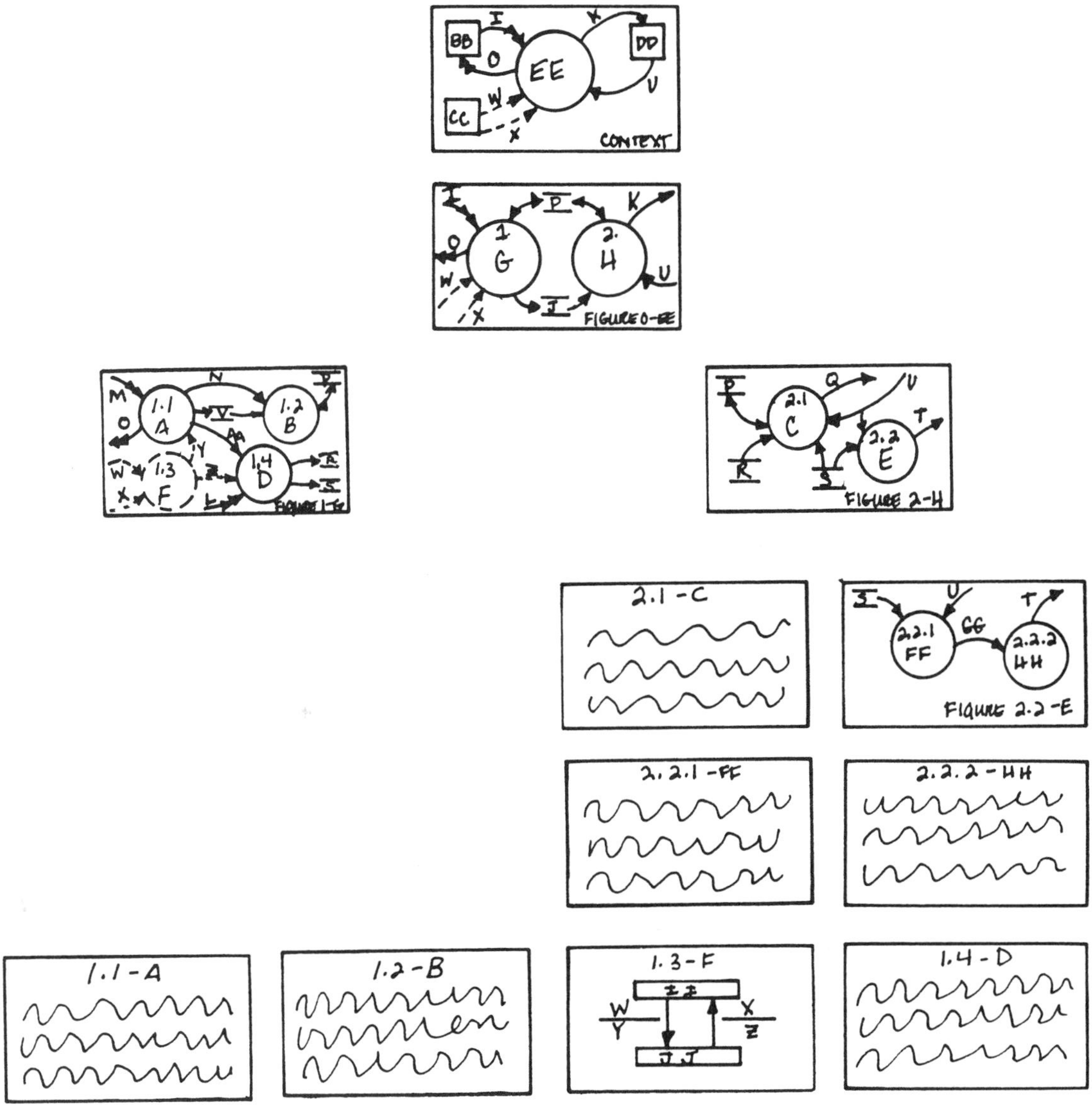

Figure 12.5. A leveled set of transformation schema.

Note that the lowest-level screens on Figure 12.5 are not transformation schemas but are *specifications* for data and control transformations. Each higher-level transformation thus summarizes the details of either a lower-level schema or a specification. The lower limit of the leveling process is reached when the logic of a transformation can be rigorously described by a specification occupying a screen or part of a screen. Specifications are needed only for the lowest level of transformations, since schemas serve as specifications for the higher-level transformations that summarize them.

Upper-level transformations, flows, and stores serve as *packagings* for the lower-level details; the packaging conventions are as follows:

- A single upper-level data transformation can summarize the details of a lower-level set of data transformations or a set containing both data and control transformations.

- A single upper-level control transformation can summarize the details of a lower-level set of control transformations.

- A single upper-level discrete data flow, continuous data flow, or event flow can summarize the details of a lower-level set of flows of the same type.

- A single upper-level data store or event store can summarize the details of a lower-level set of stores of the same type.

Note that the first packaging convention means that the conventions for separation of data and control apply only to the lowest-level schemas in a leveled set.

12.5 Numbering conventions for a leveled set

Figure 12.5 also shows a convention for numbering the screens in the leveled set. The context schema is not numbered. The next lower-level screen is numbered as figure zero, and its transformations are numbered 1, 2, 3, ... The numbering does not imply *sequencing* of the transformations but merely differentiates them. From figure zero downward, each lower-level screen carries not only the name, but also the number, of the transformation that summarizes its details. Transformations on a lower-level schema carry the number of the screen suffixed by a decimal point and another number. For example, the transformations on figure 2.2 are numbered 2.2.1, 2.2.2, and so on.

The numbering scheme is convenient because it permits rapid identification of individual screens. The number assigned to a screen also indicates its position in the overall hierarchy. Figure 2.2, for example, is three levels down from the context schema and spells out the details of transformation 2.2 on figure 2. Figure 2, in turn, is two levels down and spells out the details of transformation 2 on figure zero.

12.6 Representation of hierarchical control

Although a leveled set of transformation schemas is a hierarchy, the connections between levels inherently represent only summarization − in other words, it is a *hierarchy of representation*. However, it is possible to use event flows in conjunction with a leveled set of schemas so that the levels of the set are coincident with levels of control and so that the leveled set represents a *hierarchy of control*.

In Figure 12.6, the top screen represents the control of the entire aircraft. Event flows to the control transformation cause it to enable or disable the operation of the propulsion and navigation subsystems, which are represented in summarized form as single transformations. The middle screen, which details the operation of the propulsion system, also constitutes the next level of control. Control transformation 2.1 enables and disables the operation of the main and auxiliary engines, which are again summarized as single transformations. The bottom screen constitutes the lowest-level of control, where the individual continuous inputs and outputs of the main engine are dealt with.

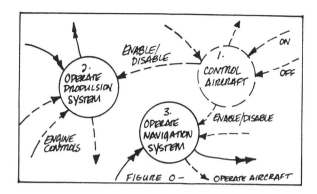

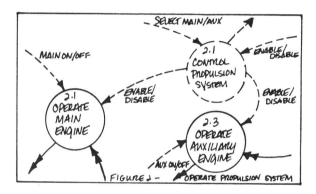

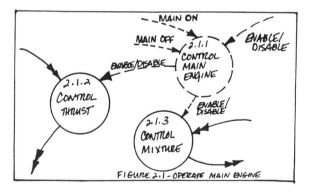

Figure 12.6. A hierarchy of control.

12.7 Leveling the data schema

The data schema needs to be partitioned for the same reasons as the transformation schema. Since the data specified in the data schema is referred to on the transformation schema through data stores, the partitioning of the transformation schema can be applied to the data schema.

However, the data schema does not partition as easily. Transformations are connected by flows, but a transformation with an attached flow or store not connected to another transformation is often easily interpretable. On the other hand, a relationship between two object types fundamentally depends on the existence of both object types. Consequently, it is not helpful to partition the data schema so that relationships are left dangling. We therefore partition the data schema by breaking it into pieces corresponding to the use of stored data by individual screens of the leveled set of transformation schemas. This scheme will cause object types to appear redundantly on portions of the data schema, but will aid understanding of the individual sub-schemas.

12.8 Summary

The leveling notation provides a method for organizing a model into presentable pieces. Controlled redundancy is introduced to hold the pieces of the model together; the upper levels of the model are entirely redundant with the lower levels.

The redundancy introduces the problem of ensuring that the redundant components are consistent. This is discussed in the next chapter.

Chapter 12: References

1. Miller, G.A. "The Magical Number Seven, Plus or Minus Two: Some Limits on Our Capacity for Processing Information." *Psychological Review, Vol. 63, No. 2* (March 1956), pp. 81-97.

2. T. DeMarco. *Structured Analysis and System Specification* (New York: Yourdon Press, 1978), pp. 71-88.

13
Integrating the Model Components

13.1 Introduction

Partitioning a system into smaller pieces allows us to think about each of the pieces independently without worrying about the details of the rest of the system.

We have partitioned the model into two projections (the transformation schema and the data schema), as well as partitioning each of those projections into components. The leveling notation introduced in the previous chapter also divides the model into pieces. For the model to be useful, there must be internal self-consistency between the components that make up each schema, between the schemas, and between the levels of the model.

13.2 Internal consistency of the transformation model

The components of the transformation schema are connected by flows. Let's begin by examining prompts that are used to activate and deactivate transformations on the schema. Since prompts are not transformed by their receivers, we can check for consistency by examining the schema alone. Fundamentally, our concern is that we can be sure we know when each transformation is active. For the transformation schema to be internally consistent, therefore, every transformation must be either triggered by a prompt-type event flow from a control transformation; enabled/disabled by a prompt-type event flow from a control transformation; or continuously active, operating on discrete or continuously available data in a time-invariant manner.

Control transformations may be checked for consistency by comparing the schematic representation of the transformation with its specification. For the transformation to be consistent, the following rules apply: All input event flows must be used as conditions, and all conditions must correspond to input event flows. All output event flows must be produced by actions, and all actions must correspond to output event flows. There must be an equivalent number of "wait on's" and "passes" on each event store used by the transformation.

Consistency for a data transformation is also defined by checking its input and output flows against its specification. However, the link between the schematic representation and the specification is less direct; we must match the specification of the transformation to the data specification as well as to the schema. For a data transformation to be consistent, the following rules apply: All data items used in the transformation specification must be declared in a data specification or must be internal to the transformation. The external data items used by the transformation must be components of input data flows. The external data items produced by the transformation must be components of output data flows.

To illustrate this, let us recall an example from Chapter 8, Specifying Data Transformations. Figure 13.1 shows the schema for the data transformation. The data specifications for the flows and stores referenced by the transformation are as follows:

Landing-Report Request = Weather Condition + Plane Type +
                         Airport Classification

Planes = {Plane}

Plane = @Plane Id + Owner Name + Plane Type

Airports = {Airport}

Airport = @Airport Id + Airport Name + Airport Classification

Landings = {Landing}

Landing = @Landing Number + Airport ref + Plane ref +
          Time of Landing

Landing Report = {Plane Id + Owner Name + Airport Id +
          Airport Name + Time of Landing +
          Weather Condition + Plane Type + Airport
          Classification}

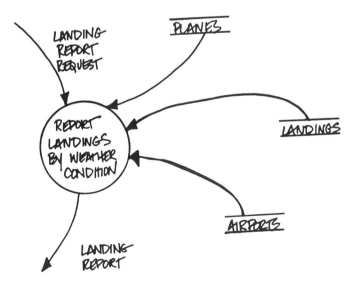

Figure 13.1. A data transformation.

We shall assume that data elements referred to here are defined elsewhere in the data specification.

The transformation specification for Report Landings by Weather Condition is:

Local terms:
> Matching Plane is a Plane where Plane Type matches Plane Type of Landing Report Request.
>
> Matching Airport is an Airport where Airport Classification matches Airport Classification of Landing Report Request.
>
> Matching Landing is a Landing where Weather Condition matches the Weather Condition of Landing Report Request and that refers to a Matching Plane and a Matching Airport.

Precondition:
> Landing Report Request occurs

Postcondition:
> Landing Report containing entries for each Matching Landing
>
> with Plane ID and Owner Name from Matching Plane
>
> and Airport ID and Airport Name from Matching Airport
>
> and Time of Landing and Weather Condition from Matching Landing.

Let us now follow the transformation specification to show consistency.

Beginning with the precondition: the Landing Report Request is defined in a data specification and as an input flow on the schema. Similarly, Landing Report is defined in a data specification and as an output flow on the schema.

Matching Plane is internally defined and refers to Plane, which is defined in a data specification. Plane contains both Plane ID and Owner Name and thus is consistent with the construction of Landing Report as shown in the postcondition. We invite the reader to check the remaining components one rainy evening to ensure that all components of the model are completely consistent.

13.3 Internal consistency of the data model

For the data schema to be internally self-consistent, we need to be able to identify uniquely each occurrence of an object type and relationship. Each object type is required to have a data element or data elements that uniquely identify each occurrence. The definition of the identifying element or elements must be included as a part of the composition specification of the object type.

Uniqueness of occurrences of an associative object type can be guaranteed by defining uniquely identifying data elements as with ordinary object types. Uniqueness can also be guaranteed by thinking of the role of the associative object type as a correlation between the uniquely identified participants in the relationship. This requires constructing the identifier from references to uniquely identified object types and possibly adding a sequencing identifying data element, if multiple occurrences are permitted.

Uniqueness of occurrences of a relationship must be guaranteed by an identifier that can be constructed from identifying instances of the participating object types. Note that identifying a Flight by references to instances of Aircraft and Pilot (Figure 13.2) is not sufficient if multiple flights can be made by a pilot in an aircraft; in this case a differentiating data element (for example, time of flight) must be added, and the relationship must become an associative object type.

An instance of subtype/supertype relationship is *by definition* uniquely identified since each subtype object type must be related to an instance of the supertype object type, and an instance of the supertype object type may be associated with one instance of one of the subtype object types.

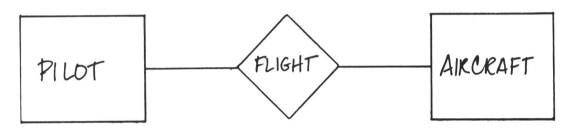

Figure 13.2. A possibly non-unique relationship.

13.4 Integrating the transformation and data schemas

The transformation schema accesses stored data as represented by data stores. To convince ourselves that the transformation schema and data schema present a consistent model, we need to make as explicit as possible the correlations between the schemas.

If we take Figure 13.3 as an example and consider a data transformation that assigns a pilot to a flight, the output flow of data is neither to the Pilot store nor the Flight store. The output flow of data is the assignment itself. We therefore represent this situation on a transformation schema as shown in Figure 13.4. Note that the relationship is shown explicitly as a store. To make the assignment correctly, the data transformation must check that both the Pilot and the Flight exist. We show this checking as input flows from the Pilots and Flights stores to the transformation.

Figure 13.3. A relationship whose instances are created by a data transformation.

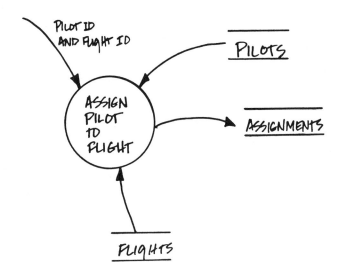

Figure 13.4. Creation of relationship instances.

In addition to creating instances of relationships as just illustrated, data transformations may use instances of relationships to trace connections between object type instances. Data transformations may also delete instances of relationships, and create, delete, or use instances of object types. In accessing object types, data transformations use and modify the data elements attributed to these object types.

Each component in the data schema must be established somehow and (presumably) exists because it is to be used. The integration of the two schemas provides us with the conceptual framework necessary to check that all data is maintained correctly by the system.

Many real-time systems contain data that describes the physical plant under control. This data is usually simply "loaded" into the data schema, and no explicit transformations exist to set its values. All other data is placed into stores by transformations. For the schemas to be consistent with respect to data establishment, all data elements must either be identified as static or have their values set as the result of a data transformation. Similarly, all object types and relationships must be identified as static or have their instances created by data transformations.

All stored data elements must be either used by a transformation or required for ad-hoc inquiries that may not have been modeled explicitly.

If every object type, relationship, and data element declared on the data schema is both established and used as defined above, the schemas can be regarded as consistent.

13.5 Internal consistency of a leveled transformation model

In a leveled set, each higher-level tranformation is simply an *abbreviation* of a lower-level schema. The activities of a transformation are defined by the transformations contained on its lower-level figure. To guarantee consistency, we must show that the net input and output flows match between the transformation and the lower-level schema. In the simplest case, the following rules apply: Each flow on the upper-level transformation must match a flow on the lower-level figure. Each store on the upper-level transformation must match a store on the lower-level figure. Each flow on the lower-level figure must *either* match a flow on the upper-level transformation *or* have its source and destination both within the figure. Each store on the lower-level figure must *either* match a store on the upper-level transformation or be used strictly within the figure.

However, the flows and stores on the upper-level transformation may also be abbreviated so as to reduce complexity. In this case, the consistency of the model must be checked through the data specification; the flow or store on the upper-level transformation must be defined as composed of the set of flows or stores on the lower-level figure.

Consider Figure 13.5, which shows a transformation and its lower-level figure. The model can be shown to be consistent if the composition of Reaction Variables is specified as Temperature + Pressure.

This process of checking the leveled model is referred to as "balancing," it can be carried out for all levels of the model and can therefore provide consistency for the entire leveled model.

13.6 Summary

The components of the schemas and their specifications must be consistent with each other to produce a useful model. In this chapter, we have provided rules for determining whether the components are indeed consistent.

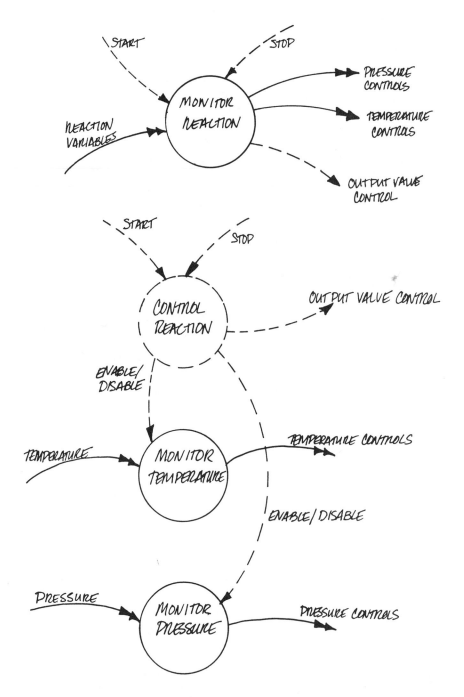

Figure 13.5. A transformation and its lower-level figure.

INDEX

Index